THE LONG BOY
AND OTHERS

WALKING UP THE HIGH STREET

Mr Johnson and I walked arm in arm up the High Street to my house in James Court: it was a dusky night: I could not prevent his being assailed by the Evening effluvia of Edinburgh.
As we marched along he grumbled in my Ear "I smell you in the dark."

Vide Journal p. 13.

Publish'd May 15th, 1786. by E. Jackson No. 14 Mary-le-bone Street, Golden Square.

THE LONG BOY

AND OTHERS

where-in will be found

A Gathering of ESSAYS,
written to Divert and Entertain
and at the same time to Instruct,
concerning several distinguished
GENTLEMEN of divers Occupation and
Wit:

SAM. JOHNSON, *Lexicographer, Poet, &c.;*
JAMES BOSWELL, *Journalist & Advocate;*
SAM. RICHARDSON, *Novelist & some-time Printer;*
HENRY FIELDING, *Magistrate & Novelist;*
T. SMOLLETT, *Writer & Surgeon;*
LAURENCE STERNE, *Clergyman & Humourist.*

newly imprinted for scholarly inspection

By B. L. REID

ATHENS

PRINTED BY
WM. LOFTIN, *Heritage Printers*, CHARLOTTE
FOR THE University of Georgia Press
MCMLXIX

ACKNOWLEDGMENTS

The author and publisher thank the editors of the following quarterlies who have graciously permitted the reprinting of the essays included in this volume:

The Hudson Review. For "Justice to *Pamela*," Vol. IX, No. 4 (Winter 1956–57). Copyright 1957 by the *Hudson Review.*

The Kenyon Review. For "Johnson's Life of Boswell," Vol. XVIII, No. 4 (Autumn 1956). Copyright 1956 by Kenyon College.

The Sewanee Review. For "Utmost Merriment, Strictest Decency: *Joseph Andrews*," Vol. LXXV, No. 4 (Autumn 1967). Copyright by the University of the South.

The Virginia Quarterly Review. For "Smollett's Healing Journey," Vol. XLI, No. 4 (Autumn 1965), and "Sterne and the Absurd Homunculus," Vol. XLIII, No. 1 (Winter 1967). Copyright 1965, 1967 by the *Virginia Quarterly Review.*

The author and publisher also gratefully acknowledge permission to quote passages from the following copyrighted material:

Boswell's London Journal, 1762–1763, edited by Frederick A. Pottle. Copyright 1950 by Yale University. Reprinted by permission of McGraw-Hill Book Company, Inc.

Five Masters: A Study in the Mutations of the Novel by Joseph Wood Krutch. Copyright 1930, 1958, by Joseph Wood Krutch. Reprinted by permission of the author.

Preface

T HE ESSAYS that follow pretend to be no more than records of my attempt to account for some of the pleasure I have found in studying certain rightly famous and familiar works of the English eighteenth century. However much we may need to sophisticate the matter professionally, the strongest lingering effect of reading these masters—Johnson, Boswell, Richardson, Fielding, Smollett, Sterne—is still that of the pleasure of their company. To know them is a lifting thing: instructive, entertaining, invigorating. The notions of heaviness, of weight and dullness, that time has attached to the period are carelessness and nonsense: this is a tonic art. No one since these masters has spoken with such lightness and brightness, such lucidity and gaiety, so round a sanity—except Jane Austen, whose career turned the century and who was really a child of their bosom, the last of their noble line.

Clear your mind of cant, said Johnson to Boswell. I always find something symptomatic in the eighteenth century's fondness for snuff: snuff is a clearer of heads. The names we attach to literary ages have a crude accuracy and much usefulness, if we stay alert to how much they fail to describe. The cant designations of the eighteenth century—the Age of Reason, the Enlightenment, the Neo-classical Age, the Augustan—all carry meaning, but it is mostly extra-literary meaning: they convey little of the real sound of the voice of genius in England at this time. The grand masters of pitch in the century, those who sound the notes to which others tune, are Pope, Johnson, and Fielding. On the face of it Johnson would seem to come closer than any other to accommodation under such rubrics as the above. He prides himself on his rationalism, his classicism, his Toryism, his enlightenment, but in such a man such essences are deeply qualified by personality and passion; he would trace his own "light," for example, straight to Scripture: he is perhaps the last True Believer. In fact Johnson's greatness of mind, of feeling, of morals rends and scatters our handy tags and envelopes.

Johnson is the greatest of all Englishmen (by no means England's greatest writer) by virtue of massive powers of person and of personality which rudely supervene classification. His greatness is cranky and individual, vulnerable yet pure, an absolute: he is easy to attack and impossible to wound. Giving orders for a family grave-marker, Johnson commands: Let the stone be deep, massy, and hard. The phrase expresses the man. Yet what a wonderful softness and availableness, an almost molten sweetness, at the center of him: think of Johnson staggering home with the sick prostitute in his arms. And not, God save us, a heavy man whatever his grand *gravitas*: walking home with Boswell through the late night streets of London, Johnson is seized with such a paroxysm of mirth upon recalling an absurdity of Langton's that he has to support himself by one of the posts at the edge of the pavement, where he "sent forth peals so loud, that in the silence of the night his voice seemed to resound from Temple-bar to Fleet-ditch."

The Age of Reason is also an Age of Mirth: that collocation is only superficially surprising. Elsewhere only in Chaucer and Shakespeare does laughter ring so free and clear, and this century as a whole must be the most risible of all: the time rocks with laughter, in many tones. The laughter of Addison and Steele is subtle, cerebrated and controlled; much of Pope's is defensive, bitter or wounding; much of Swift's is angry or grieving, broken with sobs; some of Sterne's is lewd and sly;

some of Burns's is mainly professional, local and systematic. But periodically in all of these, and steadily in Johnson, Gay, Sheridan, Goldsmith, Fielding, and Smollett, sounds the loud, clear, pure note of the century's good humor. It follows, both as cause and effect, that this is a great age of both comedy and satire.

What is the quality of light in the Enlightenment? In the imaginative literature of the century in England, the light seems to me to have little to do with science or skepticism, or with intellection at all, per se. Something about this time freed the mind and spirit of certain athletic geniuses to move with ease and confidence, and that is the light we feel: the light of brilliant sensibility, free to work and speak. Our pleasure arises from the pleasure these spirits take in their own generous moving and expressing. It is an effulgence in some sense accidental, the light of personality involved in the pleasure of circulating. This was the last age that felt free to see and say, and consequently the richness it offers is that of openness, readiness, and fullness of response, a confident adequacy of sensibility to the event. Since the eighteenth century we have complicated response but I do not know that we have improved it: since that age of originals we seem to have shrunk and dried and merely trepidated sensibility.

The real Age of Lead, it seems to me, arrived with the Romantics, when men began to believe that they were themselves fascinating and incomprehensible. The eighteenth century was the latest age to suppose that it could look at "life" and understand it. Nobody in his right mind would now write an *Essay on Man*. No doubt that kind of confidence expresses a measure of darkness rather than light: it is possible only to innocence of sorts. It is easy and perhaps necessary to call the age relatively simplistic. Yet it needs a brave time to find itself superior to a time that produced, for example, Pope and Swift and Burke and Reynolds and Congreve as well as the masters visited in this book. But I really mean to speak against invidiousness, not to encourage it, and to affirm that the effects of genius in the English eighteenth century are among the purest and richest available to us. If we approach them in their own spirit, with no defensiveness and no condescension, we see how much pleasure they felt and how much truth they told, in a triumph of style commensurate with clear vision.

B. L. Reid

March 1969
South Hadley, Massachusetts

To Robert Borgia Orlovich and the lady Ione
with thanks for ancient kindness.

SPECIAL ACKNOWLEDGMENTS

I am grateful to Mr. Fred Thompson of the University of Georgia Press for his imaginative work on the design of this book, and to Miss Susan Ganis of Toronto and points south for tasteful suggestions. My thanks go also to Mr. George Core of the University of Georgia Press for his friendly interest in my work in general and especially for his intelligent treatment of this part of it, and to Mr. Lodwick Hartley for his good wishes and good offices.

B.L.R.

*. . . just as we rose, a sailor from the vessel arrived
for us. We got all ready with dispatch. Dr. Johnson
was displeased at my bustling, and walking quickly
up and down. He said, "It does not hasten us a
bit. It is getting on horseback in a ship. All boys do
it; and you are longer a boy than others."*

—Johnson to Boswell
October 13, 1773

Johnson's Life of Boswell

"I HAVE one of the most singular minds that ever was formed," James Boswell wrote in his journal on the 8th of February in 1768; we applaud the statement, because we have long thought the same thing, and because we feel that prodigal as he is Boswell cannot be too prodigal with such evidences of his huge confessional urge and his dumbfounded narcissism. We need all these and more to understand him. Amazed as we must be at the ravelled case history of Boswell, we cannot be more amazed than Boswell himself was. Again and again his journals and letters show him wide-eyed at his own spectacle—delighted, frightened, querulous, or despairing, but always bewildered. On the eve of his departure for the continent in the summer of 1763 Boswell wrote to Sir David Dalrymple, one of the first of that series of older mentors whom he supplicated in the configuration of adolescence he never outgrew, the following ominous compound of confession, resolution, and despair:

> My great object is to attain a proper conduct in life. How sad will it be, if I turn no better than I am; I have much vivacity, which leads me to dissipation and folly. This, I think, I can restrain. But I will be moderate, and not aim at a stiff sageness and buckram correctness. I must, however, own to you, that I have at bottom a melancholy cast; which dissipation relieves by making me thoughtless, and therefore, an easier, tho' a more contemptible, animal. I dread a return of this malady. I am always apprehensive of it. . . . Tell me . . . if years do not

strengthen the mind, and make it less susceptible of being hurt? and if having a rational object will not keep up my spirits?

The same confusion of motive, lighter in tone, reappears in a letter to William Temple of 1767:

My life is one of the most romantic that I believe either you or I really know of; and yet I am a very sensible, good sort of man. What is the meaning of this, Temple? You may depend upon it, that very soon my follies will be at an end, and I shall turn out an admirable member of society.

In between these letters occurs one of the most pathetic of all Boswellian documents, his "Inviolable Plan, To be read over frequently," which is part of the second-person *retenu* journal of 1763–64, in Holland. The first paragraph of this long piece, the stratagem of a man not far from collapse, shows us as nothing else can Boswell's chronic bewilderment:

You have got an excellent heart and bright parts. You are born to a respectable station in life. You are bound to do the duties of a *Laird* of Auchinleck. For some years past you have been idle, dissipated, absurd, and unhappy. Let those years be thought of no more. You are now determined to form yourself into a man. Formerly all your resolutions were overturned by a fit of the spleen. You believed that you had a real distemper. On your first coming to Utrecht you yielded to that idea. You endured severe torment. You was pitiful and wretched. You was in danger of utter ruin. This severe shock has proved of the highest advantage. Your friend Temple showed you that idleness was your sole disease. The Rambler showed you that vacuity, gloom, and fretfulness were the causes of your woe, and that you was only afflicted as others are. He furnished you with principles of philosophy and piety to support the soul at all times. You returned to Utrecht determined. You studied with diligence. You grew quite well. This is a certain fact. You must never forget it.

For a long time, especially after Macaulay, it was fashionable to despise Boswell, and that was easy; for the past generation, after the treasures-trove of Malahide and Fettercairn, it has been fashionable to "understand" Boswell, and that is not easy at all. In fact, though the despicable data are superabundant now, it is probably harder than ever either to despise or to understand this really incredible man.

Yet our feelings about Boswell are so painful and ambiguous that they will not let us rest; they push us on toward that extravagant strangeness at the heart of the man. Why did Johnson, who did not suffer fools gladly, suffer Boswell, who had so many of the traits? What was the psychology of that incongruous relationship? All of us feel the incongruity, though we feel it less violently than Macaulay, and though we will not be tempted to reduce it as Walpole did in calling it the "story of a mountebank and his zany." Macaulay's is the intellectual-snob view of the relationship. We may easily forget, too, that there was an obverse of this: the view of Boswell's Scottish circle which held that, far from "climbing" in his pursuit of Johnson, Boswell was actually condescending disgracefully. Thus "old Touchwood Auchinleck," as Carlyle called Boswell's father, scorned his son for "taking on" with "ane that kept a schule, and ca'd it an academy"; and Margaret Boswell, as everybody knows, moved by this motive and by shame at her husband's ductility, remarked, "I have seen many a bear led by a man: but I never before saw a man led by a bear." And Boswell himself felt the incongruity in the standard form, and wrote to Sir David Dalrymple: "You will smile to think of the association of so enormous a genius with one so slender."

We will find it instructive to trace with some care the earliest motions of this friendship in the weeks between the first meeting on May 16, 1763, and Boswell's sailing for Holland on August 6. For what we find is that, after the first awful one-two to Boswell's wind in Davies' shop, Johnson is if anything more aggressively anxious than the younger man to form and sustain their union; finding Boswell still standing after the horrendous assault, Johnson in effect reaches out and gathers him into his arms. Here, briefly, is the sequence as it develops in Boswell's *London Journal.*

On the day after his meeting with the great moralist Boswell has an "agreeable congress" with a street girl named Alice Gibbs in a "snug place" in a London lane. On the 19th, at the Shakespeare's Head, he has a near miss, as "Macdonald," "a Scotch Highlander," with one woman, then scores with two: "I solaced my existence with them, one after the other, according to their seniority." Next day his "blood still thrilled with pleasure"; that evening, meeting Lady Margaret Hume, with whom he had broken an engagement, "I apologized for myself by saying that I was an odd man. She seemed to understand my worth, and said it was a pity that I should just be lost in the common stream of people here." On Saturday, May 21, he drinks tea with Temple, and attends Temple's lecture of that kind which he always seemed to enjoy almost as much as whoring:

> . . . Temple . . . was in fine frame and talked to me seriously of getting out of a course of dissipation and rattling and acquiring regularity and reserve, in order to attain dignity of character and happiness. He had much weight with me, and I resolved to be in earnest to pursue the course which he admired.

On Tuesday he meets three seasoned rounders, the "London Geniuses," Wilkes, Churchill, and Lloyd. "From this chorus, which was rather too outrageous and profane, I went and waited upon Mr. Samuel Johnson"—finding him "very solemn and very slovenly." Johnson treats him well and presses him to stay after other callers have left:

> "Sir," said I, "I am afraid that I intrude upon you. It is benevolent to allow me to sit and hear you." He was pleased with this compliment, which I sincerely paid him, and he said he was obliged to any man who visited him. I was proud to sit in such company.

There is talk of knowledge and morality. Then "He pressed me to stay a second time, which I did." Johnson sketches his own prowling habits—about the town from four in the afternoon until two in the morning. Boswell dares to wonder if this is a good use of talents, and Johnson, amazingly, accepts the censure and agrees with it. Before they part with a cordial handshake Johnson promises to visit Boswell in his lodgings. Some lines are already beginning to appear: Johnson is restless and lonely, afraid of solitude, grateful for distraction, willing to be admired; Boswell is willing to listen, willing to compliment, proud of his acquaintance, genuinely anxious for moral and intellectual buttressing. Clearly the two men are hitting it off, and gratitude is moving in both directions.

There is a good deal of rather dull sociability in these days with Boswell's worthy—too worthy—friend Temple and his younger brother Bob; but Bob shows unexpected parts when he introduces Boswell to "a Miss Temple, an exceeding pretty girl . . . kept by a man of £4,000 a year . . . very amorous, and is kind to her favourites without any views of interest." On Saturday, June 4, Boswell has a gaudy time celebrating the king's birthnight, dressing himself as a "complete blackguard" in his rowdiest clothes and "roaring along" through the town wenching and brawling, and much set up that in spite of his disguise he is everywhere recognized as a gentleman. Then on the 13th he meets Johnson again and finds him as formerly communicative and cordial. Boswell feels himself seriously edified and ennobled: "I never am with this great man without feeling myself bettered and rendered happier." Johnson takes leave of him with a handshake, bids him to call oftener and not to fear that he is troublesome, assures Boswell that he will be very glad to see him. "Can I help being vain of this?" the young man asks his journal, very reasonably.

At the Mitre on the evening of the 25th of June their talk is the most expansive and the most personal to date. There is a random literary preamble and then Boswell, as he so loved to do, opens his heart on the subject of himself: "I then told my history to Mr. Johnson, which he listened to with attention." Boswell stresses his return to Christianity after a fling at infidelity, and Johnson, "much pleased with my ingenuous open way"—and with his own skeptical youth no doubt recalled to mind—cries, "Give me your hand. I have taken a liking to you." Johnson discourses on the Christian Evidences. Boswell then opens his heart yet further: "I told him all my story"—emphasizing, apparently, his painful squirming under his father's harsh disapprobation; for Johnson offers balm for his adolescent sense of failure: " 'Sir', said he, 'your father has been wanting to make the man of you at twenty which you will be at thirty' "; and props for that huge but shaky ego of Boswell's: " 'Sir, let me tell you that to be a Scotch landlord, where you have a number of families dependent upon and attached to you, is perhaps as high a situation as humanity can arrive at.' " Johnson assures him that he need feel no special pressure in forming his plan of study. Now, feeling all this big hovering warmth where before all had been so cold and unsure, Boswell makes the crucial gestures:

> I put out my hand. "Will you really take charge of me? It is very good in you, Mr. Johnson, to allow me to sit with you thus. Had I but thought some years ago that I should pass an evening with the Authour of *The Rambler*!" These expressions were all from the heart, and he perceived that they were; and he was very complacent and said, "Sir, I am glad we have met. I hope we shall pass many evenings and mornings too together."

There is a little more talk of "authours" and "perambulation," they sit until nearly two in the morning, finish two bottles of wine, and Boswell goes home "in high exultation."

On the first of July Boswell sups with Johnson and Goldsmith at the Mitre; the literary talk is undistinguished, but Goldsmith comes out with a cardinal statement, one of those independent analyses of Boswell that we very much need to understand a part of his function for Johnson:

> He said I had a method of making people speak. "Sir," said I, "that is next best to speaking myself." "Nay," said he, "but

6

you do both." I must say indeed that if I excel in anything, it is in address and in making myself easily agreeable.

Boswell concludes, complacently, "This evening passed very well, I was very quiet and attentive."

The next meeting, July 5, is of interest only because it is the occasion of the first of Boswell's disagreements with Johnson—here, as usually, silent—on matters of literary taste. But the meeting of the following day is a famous one. Boswell has engaged Johnson and others to supper at his lodgings, but this is prevented by a violent quarrel with his landlord in consequence of a noisy party in Boswell's rooms the night before. So he assembles his company at the Mitre instead— "Mr. Samuel Johnson, Dr. Goldsmith, Mr. Ogilvie, Mr. Davies, bookseller, and Mr. Eccles, an Irish gentleman of fortune." This evening is clearly the crown, socially and intellectually, of Boswell's life to date, and he is quietly proud of the figure he makes:

> I was well dressed and in excellent spirits, neither muddy nor flashy. I sat with much secret pride, thinking of my having such a company with me. I behaved with ease and propriety, and did not attempt at all to show away; but gently assisted conversation by those little arts which serve to make people throw out their sentiments with ease and freedom.

There is fine random talk of literature and politics, and then Johnson gets off his sally: ". . . the noblest prospect that a Scotsman ever sees is the road which leads him to England." Boswell reproves, silently, Johnson's "want of taste in laughing at the wild grandeur of nature," and is moved to a—silent —fulsome apostrophe to that wild grandeur: "O Arthur Seat, thou venerable mountain!" etc. Boswell closes his account of the evening with another bit of that self-gratulation which, in the sequel, turns so funny and so heartbreaking:

> This evening I have had much pleasure. That is being truly rich. And riches are only a good because men have a pleasure in

spending them, or in hoarding them up. I have received this night both instruction and pleasure.

On the 14th of July Boswell and Johnson are at the Mitre again. Boswell wonders why he gets on so well with Johnson —"You and I, Sir, are very good companions"—and so poorly with his father, when the two men are of an age. Johnson lays the difference to his own cosmopolitanism as compared to the provincialism of Lord Auchinleck. Then, seeking as always the principle behind the particular, he comes up with one of the more acute of his "general truths": "Besides, there must always be a struggle between a father and son, while the one aims at power and the other at independency." Boswell passes on "some very pretty compliments, which pleased him much," from Sir David Dalrymple to Johnson. Johnson advises him to keep a journal of his life, "fair and undisguised," and is glad to hear that Boswell has already done so for some time. Boswell feels a quick access of pride at having anticipated the moralist: "And now, O my journal! art thou not highly dignified? Shalt thou not flourish tenfold?" But it is clear that Johnson conceives a journal as a matter for the closet only: "He said indeed that I should keep it private, and that I might surely have a friend who would burn it in case of my death." Boswell, fortunately for us, congenitally unsympathetic to all this huddling up and secrecy, shrinks from the idea of burning: "I rather encourage the idea of having it carefully laid up among the archives of Auchinleck." When they part, after two bottles of port between them, Boswell says, "He took me cordially by the hand and said, 'My dear Boswell! I do love you very much.' "

On the 19th Boswell has a look at Johnson's library, with its books in dust and confusion, its "chymical" apparatus, and its scattering of manuscript leaves. Next day he invites Johnson, Dr. Blair, and Dempster to supper in his chambers. Johnson talks a great deal of hard-headed pragmatic morality, much of it on his favorite subject of "subordination." Dr.

Blair leaves early and reproves Jamie *sotto voce* at the door: "There are few people in Edinburgh who would keep company with this man." But Boswell will have none of this, preferring the reverse snobbery with its nice distinction of himself: ". . . sure I am there are very few people in Edinburgh with whom Mr. Johnson would keep company." Again this evening he finds his own conduct satisfactory: "I behaved extremely well tonight. I was attentive and cheerful and manly." After Johnson leaves, Boswell, full of reflected powers, continues to beat down Dempster on the issue of subordination: "He appeared to me a very weak man; and I exulted at the triumph of sound principles over sophistry."

On the evening of the 22nd in a room at the Turk's Head, the older man offers one of the revealing analyses of the relationship:

> Mr. Johnson said he loved the acquaintance of young people. "Because," said he, "in the first place, I don't like to think myself turning old. In the next place, young acquaintances must last longest, if they do last; and in the next place, young men have more virtue than old men. They have more generous sentiments in every respect. I love the young dogs of this age: they have more wit and humour and knowledge of life than we had."

Boswell and Johnson discover yet another meeting ground, their common susceptibility to deep depression or "hypochondria." There is a pleasant interchange of symptoms. Johnson reverts, obsessively, to the subject of subordination. Then he expresses a desire to perambulate the Hebrides with Boswell, and seconds that with unusual words of kindness:

> He said, "There are few people whom I take so much to as you"; and when I talked of leaving England, he said (with an affection that almost made me cry), "My dear Boswell! I should be very unhappy at parting, did I think we were not to meet again."

On the 25th Boswell tries his fledgling oratorical powers

at the Robin Hood Society, with applause from the audience but little from himself: he is full of self-doubt. On the 28th he records that he has met Peggy Doig, the mother of his first illegitimate child, in town, and read her a lecture on loose behavior. That evening he and Johnson again share a room at the Turk's Head, and after some discourse of Swift and Addison the talk shifts to a more momentous subject:

> We then talked of Me. He said that I was very forward in knowledge for my age; that a man had no reason to complain who held a middle place and had many below him; and that perhaps I had not six above me. Perhaps not one. He did not know one. This was very high. I asked him, if he was my father, and if I did well at the law, if he would be pleased with me. "Sir," said he, "I should be pleased with you whatever way of life you followed, since you are now in so good a way. Time will do all that is wanting. Indeed, when you was in the irreligious way, I should not have been pleased with you." I returned him many thanks for having established my principles.

Boswell presses for further advice on his Utrecht studies, and Johnson suggests that they "make a day" of the subject on Saturday at Greenwich. At the end of the day Boswell pauses once more to note his delight and wonderment at Johnson's continued intimacy: "It must be something curious for the people in the Turk's Head Coffee-house to see this great man and poor Me so often together by ourselves. My vanity is much flattered."

Saturday is marked first by the touching colloquy with the boat boy, so nicely highlighted in the *Life*: "He then said to the boy, 'What would you give, Sir, to know about the Argonauts?' 'Sir,' said he, 'I would give what I have.' The reply pleased Mr. Johnson much. . . ." Standing on the banks of the Thames, Boswell pulls from a strategic pocket a copy of *London: A Poem*, reads from it, then "literally" stoops to kiss the sacred ground. Johnson's specific advice on studies turns out to be sufficiently cloudy: ". . . he run over the grand scale of human knowledge, advised me to select some particular branch to excel in, but to have a little of every kind"—a major and many minors. The day's capstone is glorious: Johnson proposes of his own accord to see the young man off for Europe. " 'I will go down with you to Harwich.' This prodigious mark of his affection filled me with gratitude and vanity." Well it might: for the sedentary, citified Johnson, here was a heroic condescension. But Johnson's largesse is not yet done; he expresses a desire to be with the young laird at Auchinleck: "I must be there, and we will live in the Old Castle; and if there is no room remaining, we will build one."

Boswell spends most of Tuesday, August 2, in Johnson's company, the forenoon in his own chambers, tea with Mrs. Williams in Bolt Court—another milestone—and supper at the Turk's Head. He has been for some days in a melancholy fit for fear of the European trial, but this evening he finds that "Mr. Johnson filled my mind with so many noble and just sentiments that the Demon of Despondency was driven away." Next evening they sup again at the same inn, but Boswell's head is so heavy from having sat up all the previous night that even Johnson can barely keep him awake.

The *London Journal* closes on this sleepy note, and for an account of the last of these great days we must turn to the *Life*. The two men take coach for Harwich in the early morning of August 5. For our purposes the only significant passage of the journey is Johnson's open guying of Boswell before his fellow passengers as a young man who has already been idle in Edinburgh, Glasgow, and London and is now going off to be idle in Utrecht. Boswell shows himself rather pained. Before they retire for the night at Colchester Johnson resumes his guying, borrowing a metaphor from a moth which has just burnt itself in their candle flame to chide Boswell for "fanciful apprehension of unhappiness": "That creature was its own tormentor, and I believe its name was Boswell." Next day Johnson performs his famous athletic refutation of Berkeley by kicking the stone outside the church in Harwich:

"I refute it *thus*." This sets the stage with a nice emphasis for the closing scene:

> My reverend friend walked down with me to the beach, where we embraced and parted with tenderness, and engaged to correspond by letters. I said, 'I hope, Sir, you will not forget me in my absence.'

> JOHNSON. 'Nay, Sir, it is more likely you should forget me, than that I should forget you.' As the vessel put out to sea, I kept my eyes upon him for a considerable time, while he remained rolling his majestick frame in his usual manner: and at last I perceived him walk back into the town, and he disappeared.

So ends the first phase of the amazing friendship, and it is time to stop and take stock. These first weeks have been definitive. Our quick purview suggests matter for a number of hypotheses as to what has essentially taken place; later we may go on to test these hypotheses in the larger scene of the ensuing twenty years. One conviction that has already moved beyond hypothesis into certainty is that Boswell did not arrogantly impose himself upon an unwilling Johnson, as the *cliché* has long held: it is perfectly clear that for reasons which we must determine Boswell's company was at least as welcome to Johnson as Johnson's was to Boswell. Handshakes, embraces, and repeated overt acts and spoken assurances, most of them unsolicited, show us that beyond doubt.

Why was Boswell welcome? Much of the answer lies in the peculiarities of the Johnsonian psyche, but that joined to the peculiarities of the interval in which the young man made his appearance. For Boswell came to Johnson in the year after the crown pension of three hundred pounds had set him permanently free of his besetting fear of poverty, free of the need to accept any more of the onerous hackwork that had kept him alive thus far, and free thereby to indulge expansively his three most notable personal traits—

his love of indolence, his love of talk, and his fear of loneliness. Boswell, with his endless willingness to sit, to saunter, and to listen, answered perfectly to all three. He had arrived at precisely the time when Johnson, who "loved to fold his legs and have out his talk," was secure at last to do so. "*Amici fures temporis*," Johnson quotes at one time: "Friends are the thieves of time"; after 1763 Johnson wanted his time stolen, and Boswell was a patient and cunning thief.

But Boswell had ability to match his presumptuousness. Johnson's case was not so desperate that he must devote long hours to any tiresome man. Boswell was, quite simply, a genius of social intercourse. "A very *clubable* man," Johnson was to call him later; and we have seen Goldsmith's encomium. Adam Smith praised his "facility of manner," and Burke, Reynolds, and even Mrs. Thrale noted the same virtue. His sociable behavior may have been his supreme creative act. Boswell was not merely an enormous ear, as we sometimes feel in the *Life*, or a question-machine, as we feel at other times; he was a really brilliant social catalyst, one who could make others precipitate and decant the pleasurable talk that was in them, a master of "those little arts which serve to make people throw out their sentiments with ease and freedom." Johnson, who loved to talk but required it to be elicited, placed a just value on Boswell's graceful art. And Boswell could talk himself, he was not a fool and he was not dumb. Goldsmith has phrased the matter for us: "Nay, said he, but you do both." Boswell, let us say, had come to the right place at the right time with the right equipment.

The discrepancy in the ages of the two men is responsible for much of the seeming incongruity of the union, but also for much of its special intimate warmth. Boswell was twenty-three, Johnson fifty-three: one thinks at once, Johnson was old enough to be his father. Exactly, Boswell and Johnson think so too: it is a note that recurs often. That Boswell sought a father-substitute in the older man is a commonplace and accurate observation. He is in flight all his life from the father Lord Auchinleck insisted on being and in search of the father Lord Auchinleck refused to be. His list is long: Lord Kames, David Hume, Sir Alexander Dick, Sir David Dalrymple, General Paoli, Sir John Pringle, Voltaire, Rousseau—and Johnson; Boswell's most significant friendships are with men of this generation, and he always approached them filially. And it is touching to find him putting to Temple, his closest confidant of his own age, the same wistful question he asked of Johnson: "Temple, if I was your son, would you be pleas'd with me?" It seems to me almost equally clear that Johnson sought in Boswell the son he had never had. That he took pleasure, vicariously, in the spectacle of youth he explicitly tells us: "I love the young dogs of this age"; and his obsessive fear of death was calmed a bit by the young vitality around him: "I don't like to think myself turning old." He felt a real kindness in a young man's eagerness for his company. Johnson's posture to Boswell is more fatherly than it is anything else—in its indulgence, its concern to teach, its affectionateness, and in the sadness of its ultimate disappointment. Johnson and Boswell anticipate, stiffly, the wry comedy of Leopold Bloom and Stephen Dedalus.

Boswell, then, played the son's part nicely by asking Johnson to be the things that, at least for the time, he took pleasure in being—confessor, moral guide, intellectual mentor, disciplinarian: in a word, the configuration of the Compleat Father. Other motives, too, there are in abundance, less interesting and on the whole less worthy: such shared crotchets as superstitiousness and hypochondria; Boswell's desire for distinction and Johnson's power and willingness to confer it; Johnson's fondness for flattery and Boswell's ability to confer it; Boswell's need as a spectacular sinner to be saved and Johnson's evangelical desire to save him. But the crucial motives of the union are the confessed social relationship and the half-confessed familial one.

There are texts which show that Johnson's regard did not cease when Boswell went abroad. As the years passed the feeling warmed at times to love, rose at times to respect, and became complicated at last by an impatience close to disgust at Boswell's habits; yet it never altered in a degree that we can call radical. The second of his letters to Boswell on the continent testifies convincingly to his undiminished affection in January 1766:

> . . . nothing has lessened either the esteem or love with which I dismissed you at Harwich. Both have been increased by all that I have been told of you by yourself or others; and when you return, you will return to an unaltered, and, I hope, unalterable friend. . . . I long to see you, and to hear you; and hope that we shall not be so long separated again.

Just before the Scotch tour Johnson sends a brief note reproving Boswell's fulsomeness but concluding, "Think only when you see me, that you see a man who loves you, and is proud and glad that you love him."

Two years later the expression, though qualified as the later letters tend to be by distaste for Boswell's anxiousness and a progressive despair at his morals, is still one of fundamentally unshaken affection:

> Never, my dear Sir, do you take it into your head to think that I do not love you; you may settle yourself in full confidence both of my love and my esteem; I love you as a kind man, I value you as a worthy man, and I hope in time to reverence you as a man of exemplary piety. I hold you, as Hamlet has it, "in my heart of hearts". . . .

Near the end of Boswell's annual visit in 1777 Johnson speaks to him in the same vein, wearied by his pleas for reassurance but still unequivocally willing to supply it: "My regard for you is greater almost than I have words to express; but I do not choose to be always repeating it; write it down in the first leaf of your pocket-book, and never doubt of it again." In the spring of the year before Johnson's death Boswell finds him ill at Mrs. Thrale's, applies the balm of his good company, and is told that his presence is as grateful as ever: "You must be as much with me as you can. You have done me good. You cannot think how much better I am since you came in." This is twenty years after the first meeting.

Now, if Johnson's words alone are not enough to make our point, we may adduce his actions—a quick catalog of his embraces: "He embraced me cordially"; "I went with him to his door where he embraced me and blessed me"; "He embraced me and said, 'Fare you well. God bless you for Jesus Christ's sake' "; "He took me in his arms, and said with solemn fervour, 'God bless you for Jesus Christ's sake' "; " . . . he hug'd you to him like a sack, and grumbl'd, 'I hope we shall pass many years of regard together' "; "He took me all in his arms and kist me on both sides of the head." Even after we have discounted for eighteenth-century fervency, we have to say that these are testaments of a deep and constant tenderness.

It would be foolish to argue that the relationship had in no way decayed with the passage of time; but the essential decay, it seems to me, occurs not in Johnson's love but in the fibres of Boswell the man. Long before Johnson's death in 1784 Boswell was firmly fixed in the syndrome of inner and outer failure, and that radical slackness, though we scarcely feel it in the *Life*, had loosened and dulled, not his love or Johnson's, but Boswell's basic hold on life, his zeal and his energy, his power to keep that love the warm and active thing it began by being.

When Boswell first called at his chambers, we remember, Johnson said to him, "Sir, I am obliged to any man who visits me"; and near the end of the *Life* Boswell recalls this late tribute: "Boswell, I think I am easier with you than with almost any body." In those two brief statements, I suspect, lies the simple secret of Boswell's value to Johnson: the first expressing something in addition to a perfunctory courtesy—

Johnson's almost pathetic need of the constant distraction of human company; the second expressing a quiet gratitude for the special kind of company Boswell so faithfully provided. It was on the basis of such a need on Johnson's part and such an endowment on Boswell's part that Johnson was moved to say, as Dudley Long reported, "Sir, if I were to lose Boswell, it would be like a limb amputated."

If Johnson were ever going to depreciate Boswell it would be, one suspects, to Mrs. Thrale—considering the terms of his intimacy with her, and considering the rivalry between his "Mistress" and his Boswell. Thus it is illuminating to follow a series of brief references to Boswell in a group of letters to Mrs. Thrale from Ashbourne in the fall of 1777. Note that every reference is open and approving: On September 13 he writes, "Boswell, I believe, is coming . . . I shall be glad to see him." On the 15th, "Last night came Boswell. I am glad that he is come. He seems to be very brisk and lively. . . ." On the 18th, "Boswell is with us in good humour; and plays his part with his usual vivacity." (On this the saturnine Baretti comments, "That is, he makes more noise than anybody in company, talking and laughing loud.") On the 25th Johnson closes the episode, "Boswell is gone. . . . He has been gay and good-humored in his usual way. . . ." (Baretti sneers, "That is, in his noisy and silly way.") When Boswell himself came to read Johnson's letters in Mrs. Thrale's edition in 1788 he reacted with a sense of shock and deep disenchantment—deeper than we, lacking Boswell's lofty expectations, can find strictly logical. His response is, in fact, a clear indication both of his waspish animosity to Mrs. Thrale and of the sad late confusions of his mind, and we should read it now for such evidences.

> I was disappointed a good deal, both in finding less able and less brilliant writing than I expected, and in having a proof of his fawning on a woman whom he did not esteem, because he had luxurious living in her husband's house; and in order that this

fawning might not be counteracted, treating me and other friends much more lightly than we had reason to expect. This publication cooled my warmth of enthusiasm for "my illustrious friend" a good deal. I felt myself degraded from the consequence of an ancient Baron to the state of an humble attendant on an Authour; and what vexed me, thought that my collecting so much of his conversation had made the World shun me as a dangerous companion.

His complaint is not wholly lacking in justice: Johnson's letters are far less brilliant than one has a right to expect—but Johnson hated to write letters; Boswell's assiduousness in "collecting" and his candor in publishing had indeed closed doors to him, inevitably—but his own dissoluteness had closed more; Johnson's references to Boswell in his letters are indeed less eulogistic than his references elsewhere—yet only once or twice does he express himself in a way that we or Boswell could call deprecatory or patronizing. After Mrs. Thrale had read the manuscript which was to become the *Journal of a Tour to the Hebrides*, Johnson wrote to her, "You never told me, and I omitted to enquire, how you were entertained by Boswell's Journal. One would think the man had been hired to be a spy upon me." The problem of interpretation there is one of tone; Johnson may have been simply commenting, with light irony, upon Boswell's industry, as the succeeding sentence in fact suggests: "He was very diligent, and caught opportunities of writing from time to time." A more genuinely patronizing reference occurs in a letter written near the end of the Scotch tour; ironically, Johnson probably meant this as his handsomest compliment to Boswell in all the letters: "Boswell will praise my resolution and perseverance; and I shall in return celebrate his good humour and perpetual cheerfulness. He has better faculties than I had imagined; more justness of discernment; and more fecundity of images." "Than I had imagined" does suggest a curious illumination after ten years' acquaintance; it suggests that Johnson had held Boswell's serious parts in a rather light estimate all that time, and that now he suddenly realizes he has long undervalued that side of him.

Johnson never tired of Boswell as a companion of his travels—surely one of the most acid tests of friendship. He makes this repeatedly clear. There is the formal tribute in the first paragraph of his *Journey to the Western Islands of Scotland*:

> . . . finding in Mr. Boswell a companion, whose acuteness would help my inquiry, and whose gaiety of conversation and civility of manners are sufficient to counteract the inconveniences of travel, in countries less hospitable than we have passed.

But more telling is such an unstudied statement as the following—made eleven years after the tour and only a few months before his death: "Boswell has a great mind to draw me to Lichfield, and as I love to travel with him, I have a mind to be drawn. . . ." To Mrs. Knowles he phrased the same judgment in terms of superlatives: "If you knew his merit as well as I do, you would say a great deal; he is the best travelling companion in the world." Finally, it is suggestive to compare the pleasure Johnson found with Boswell in Scotland with his dyspepsia on the continental tour with the Thrales.

Happily Boswell has left us a vignette in his *Journal of a Tour to the Hebrides* which shows us pretty precisely what were his services as a traveling companion to Johnson. He is both expert steward and unobtrusive master of the revels:

> . . . I must take some credit from my assiduous attention to him, and the happy art which I have of contriving that he shall be easy wherever he goes, that he shall not be asked twice to eat or drink anything (which always disgusts him), that he shall be provided with water at his meals, and many such little things, which, if not attended to, would fret him. I have also an admirable talent of leading the conversation: I do not mean leading as in an orchestra, by playing the first fiddle, but leading as one does in examining a witness: starting topics, and making the company pursue them. Mr. Johnson appeared to me like a great

mill, into which a subject is thrown to be ground. That is the test of a subject. But indeed it requires fertile minds to furnish materials for this mill.

And near the end of the tour he gives us a scrap of action from a Glasgow scene which dramatizes the whole relationship in a flash:

> . . . I, having a letter to write, left my fellow-traveller with Messieurs Foulis. Though good and ingenious men, they had that unsettled speculative mode of conversation which is offensive to a man regularly taught at an English school and university. I found that instead of listening to the dictates of the sage, they had teased him with questions and doubtful disputations. He came in a flutter to me and desired I might come back again, for he could not bear these men. "O ho! sir," said I, "you are flying to me for refuge;" . . . He answered, with quick vivacity, "It is of two evils choosing the least." I was delighted with this flash bursting from the cloud which hung upon his mind, closed my letter directly, and joined the company.

Which is another useful dash of salt in the pudding I continue to make unnaturally sweet.

We need to turn at last to the less happy portions of the story and to fill out the picture of Johnson as Compleat Father. In one of his letters to Temple, Boswell offers a bit of ingenuousness, both pathetic and delightful, which can stand as a tentative microcosm of this history: "He is to buy for me a chest of books of his chusing off stalls, and I am to read more and drink less." Johnson sent the books, and when Boswell got around to opening them weeks later he scorned them as "a numerous and miscellaneous *Stall Library*, thrown together at random"; he then proceeded to read less and drink more. The fact is, if we tabulate Johnson's paternal utterances, his advice, his censure, and his approbation, we soon see that whereas he never ceased to love Boswell as a partner in talk or travels, he found little to approve in twenty years' experience of Boswell as son and pupil. We know perfectly well why this was true: there was little for anyone to approve in Boswell's life outside his wonderful service as Good Fellow. It is only too well known, on the testimony of the *Life* and the *Boswell Papers*, that Johnson made a parlor sport out of "tossing" Boswell, as the latter called it. But that is not very important: he was only a little fonder of tossing Boswell than of tossing anyone else, and Boswell was temperamentally and philosophically very well able to bear it. He put the matter in what is after all a very just perspective:

> Speaking of Mr. Johnson's roughness to me at times I told her [Mrs. Stuart] that he said to me at Edinburgh, before Dr. Blair and some more, that he reckoned the day on which he and I became acquainted one of the happiest days of his life. "Now," said I, "what a number of little attacks will it take to counterbalance this. If he gives me a hundred thousand pounds, and he takes from me a shilling, or even a guinea, now and then, what a time will it take before he gets his great gift back again." "Nay," said she, "he never can take it from you."

We need not take it much more seriously than Boswell does when Johnson regrets that he had not been available for the *Dunciad* or advises him to get his head "fumigated." In the scale of the hundred-thousand-pound praise such peckish insult or bearish wit, in moments of passing pique or petty tyrannizing, makes little organic difference. What we rather want to know is how Johnson thought of Boswell when he was working most seriously at the subject.

We have the magnificent letter which Johnson wrote to Boswell in Utrecht in December 1763. Everything that follows is, sadly, a footnote to that letter, and on a descending scale moving toward weariness or despair—not so much recorded in overt statement as implied in perfunctory phrase or merely formal tone. We can follow this progress, but we need first to recall that august document, the Utrecht letter. Johnson is responding to two letters of Boswell's, the first of which especially had been a long whine of fear and discontent. Having now Boswell's continental journal, we see his actual shivering misery, something very close to madness, and it is a good deal easier for us to forgive his moaning abjectness than it can have been for Johnson. After noticing Boswell's first letter in phrases of dignified contempt—"The first, indeed, gave me an account so hopeless of the state of your mind, that it hardly admitted or deserved an answer"—Johnson then settles in an attitude that mingles austere kindness and elevated counsel in one of the most imposing things ever to come from his pen. The easy rein with which Johnson had promised to ride in those days in London has visibly tightened; the new counsel, while it is not much more specific, is vastly more stringent. The letter should be re-read in any case; but perhaps one passage near the close can sufficiently suggest its tone and tenor:

> Let all such fancies, illusive and destructive, be banished henceforward from your thoughts for ever. Resolve, and keep your resolution; choose, and pursue your choice. If you spend this day in study, you will find yourself still more able to study tomorrow; not that you are to expect that you shall at once obtain a complete victory. Depravity is not very easily overcome. Resolution will sometimes relax, and diligence will sometimes be interrupted; but let no accidental surprise or deviation, whether short or long, dispose you to despondency. Consider these failings as incident to all mankind. Begin again where you left off, and endeavour to avoid the seducements that prevailed over you before.

Johnson's strictures on Boswell's social behavior are among his shallower rebukes, and we can dispose of those fairly quickly. Society meant for Johnson basically conversation, and by the nice distinction he draws between conversation and "talk" we know well enough what were his expectations in social intercourse: "No, Sir; we had *talk* enough, but no *conversation*; there was nothing *discussed*." There were, of course, the interdicted subjects, such as America, or "bawdy," or death. But three habits in conversation were anathema to Johnson, and he found Boswell on occasion guilty of all three:

excessive use of personal applications, excessive use of a question-and-answer form, and excessive or self-conscious bookishness, especially to cover a poverty of original ideas. At one point he was moved to compliment Boswell by saying, "You and I do not talk from books." But Boswell's sin on this head was poverty rather than excess, and on another occasion Johnson called attention to his inadequate bookish foundation in general truth: "Said Mr. Johnson: 'I wish you had read more books. The foundations must be laid by reading. General principles must be had from books.'" Johnson's distaste for personal references was partly philosophical, partly temperamental: he sought principles larger than personalities, and he objected to having himself made a datum in any demonstration. The strength of his feeling about this is shown by the strength of his rebukes:

> "Sir, you put an end to all argument when you introduce your opponent himself. Have you no better manners? There is *your want*."

> "You have but two topicks, yourself and me, and I'm sick of both. Who of our club talks of me thus, makes me a constant topick?"

His dislike for repeated questioning was equally violent. When Boswell has been too persistent Johnson says to him, "This now is such stuff as I used to talk to my mother, when I first began to think myself a clever fellow; and she ought to have whipt me for it." And again:

> I will not be put to the *question*. Don't you consider, Sir, that these are not the manners of a gentleman? I will not be baited with *what*, and *why*; what is this? what is that? why is a cow's tail long? why is a fox's tail bushy?

Langton told Boswell privately that Johnson had said to him, "When Boswell gets wine, his conversation consists all of questions," and that is a statement which carries us neatly from his venial to his mortal sins.

Toward Boswell's drinking and his whoring Johnson sometimes displayed a kind of easy-going complacency that is rather
surprising. Boswell showed his own moral fibres at their
slackest in seeking to manipulate Johnson so as to secure from
him pronouncements which could be rationalized as palliative
if not approving. He was perfectly sensible of the irony of
his own behavior when a professed follower of the Rambler.
As he says to himself en route to Ashbourne to meet the great
moralist in 1777, after dallying with the chambermaids of
three successive wayside inns, " 'How inconsistent,' thought
I, 'is it for me to be making a pilgrimage to see Dr. Johnson,
and licentiously loving wenches by the way.' " But Johnson
could, as I say, respond very lightly to such peccadilloes. One
of the most delightful exchanges in the *Life* is that with
Wilkes which takes place in the scene of Boswell's greatest
social coup, the fabulous dinner at Dilly's in 1776:

> JOHNSON. (to Mr. Wilkes) "You must know, Sir, I lately took
> my friend Boswell and shewed him genuine civilised life in an
> English provincial town. I turned him loose at Lichfield, my
> native city, that he might see for once real civility: for you
> know he lives among savages in Scotland, and among rakes in
> London." WILKES. "Except when he is with grave, sober, de-
> cent people like you and me." JOHNSON. (smiling) "And we
> ashamed of him."

Boswell's drinking is a considerable problem on the Scottish
tour. He helps make way with four bowls of punch at Coirechatachan, falls into bed at five in the morning, and awakes
at noon with a bursting head and shame at his unseemly course:
"I thought it very inconsistent with that conduct which I
ought to maintain while the companion of the Rambler."
Yet Johnson is only indulgently sardonic:

> 'What, drunk yet?' His tone of voice was not that of severe
> upbraiding; so I was relieved a little. 'Sir,' said I, 'they kept me
> up.' He answered, 'No, you kept them up, you drunken dog.'
> This he said with good-humoured English pleasantry. Soon

afterwards, Coirechatachan, Coll, and other friends assembled around my bed. Corry had a brandy bottle and glass with him, and insisted I should take a dram. 'Ay,' said Dr. Johnson, 'fill him drunk again. Do it in the morning that we may laugh at him all day. It is a poor thing for a fellow to get drunk at night, and skulk to bed, and let his friends have no sport.' Finding him thus jocular, I became quite easy. . . . When I rose, I went into Dr. Johnson's room, and taking up Mrs. Mackinnon's prayer book. I opened it at the twentieth Sunday after Trinity, in the epistle for which I read, "And be not drunk with wine, wherein there is excess." Some would have taken this as a divine interposition.

Later in the tour Johnson faces the matter a good deal more dourly: "Mr. Johnson . . . very justly reproved me for taking the *scalck* or dram every morning. He said, 'For shame!' and that it was now really become serious. It was lucky that he corrected me." And later still we see the thing grown into a formula, with Johnson pessimistically admonitory and Boswell skulking but resolved to have his liquor:

Another bowl was made. Mr. Johnson had gone to bed as the first was finished, and had admonished me, "Don't drink any more *poonch*." I must own that I was resolved to drink more, for I was by this time a good deal intoxicated; and I gave no answer, and slunk away from him, with a consciousness of my being brutish and yet a determination to go somewhat deeper. What I might have done I know not. But luckily before I had tasted the second bowl, I grew very sick, and was forced to perform the operation that Antony did in the Senate house, if Cicero is to be credited. . . .

I am afraid that this is nearer to the norm of things. That Johnson was doomed to fail in his effort to reform Boswell the drunkard shows clearly in this journal entry for April 15, 1772: Boswell asks, "Would you not, Sir, allow a man oppressed with care to drink, and make himself merry?" and Johnson replies, "Yes, if he sat next *you*." Boswell, unshaken, babbles on:

I never was disturbed. I know Mr. Johnson so well, and delight
in his grand explosions, even when directed against myself, so
much, that I am not at all hurt.

That Johnson understood the psychology and the classic pattern of the self-dramatizing drunk is clear from a passage
such as this in Boswell's journal:

> HE. ". . . What hinders your reformation is that you are always
> speaking of it: 'General Paoli took my promise, and Dr. John-
> son approves.' Now consider that nobody really cares, only they
> want a topick for conversation. No. Go to Scotland, and say,
> simply, I've left off wine.' " (Thrale had told him I said I had
> been drunk 12 times since I came to London.) I was humbled.

One other brief note from the 1776 visit suggests that
whereas he understood the outlines of Boswell's case, Johnson
probably had not seen all his symptoms in full flower: "He
bid me divert melancholy by every means but drinking. I
thought then of women, but no doubt he no more thought
of my indulging in licentious copulation than of my stealing."
Boswell was all his life a man in frantic flight from recurrent
grinding depression, melancholia, or "hypochondria"—the
"English Malady" in virulent form. His escape he sought by
three main routes: alcohol, women, and the company of the
intellectual great. He could not do without any of the three,
yet he could not bear the thought that his vices, women and
wine, must sooner or later deny him his virtue, the cultivation
of intelligence; so of course he tried to travel his three routes
concurrently, and to deceive Johnson adequately while doing
so. Thus it is significant that there are relatively so few recorded pronouncements of Johnson's on the subject of Boswell's profligacy. Either Boswell has suppressed some of Johnson's utterances—which would be very unlike him—or else
he somehow managed to hide from Johnson the full heroic
proportions of his sinning. If Boswell could believe after thir-
teen years' acquaintance that Johnson still did not know of his

habitual whoring, then it seems likely that he had indeed been both lucky and successful in shielding himself from the full baleful glare of Johnson's eye. We know of his repeated vinous indiscretions in Johnson's company; yet he seems to have stopped those always short of the displays of wallowing disgracefulness which were part of his symptomatology at its lowest depths. Boswell's compulsive sexuality is a gaudy sight to the reader of his journals, but Johnson did not read those. Yet he was constantly begging Johnson for palliative opinions—in the abstract—of "fornication" and "concubinage." And there is one suggestive lacuna in Volume XI of the *Boswell Papers* which indicates, as an editorial note hazards, that he may on one occasion have braved the Rambler's full wrath—and received it. On Good Friday and Easter Day— he was not one to brood about proprieties—he was steering the talk persistently in the direction of these favorite subjects; but ten pages, containing the Johnsonian record for Sunday and the complete record for Monday and Tuesday, are torn from the journal; and when it resumes the entry indicates that an explosion of some size has taken place. Perhaps April 7, 1776, was the day Boswell got what was coming to him; had he dared something like a full confession on that day?

In any case, Johnson's increasingly serious view of Boswell's dissipations is already clear; as time passed his response hardened and dulled into sadness, boredom, and disillusionment. He grew more and more hopeless of doing anything about the decaying man, and less and less willing to be troubled with his sick complaints, usually centering about his miserable melancholy. Johnson seems to have grouped Boswell's sins of depression and profligacy under the single inclusive head of failure of manliness; his diagnosis was probably accurate clinically if not terminologically. For Boswell's failures really were those of anachronism—perpetuating the fears and the susceptibilities of adolescence into manhood. "You are longer a boy than others," Johnson told him during the tour, meaning only a passing reproof; we can accept it as the richest possible text.

Johnson's disenchantment parallels, as we now know, the slow collapse of Boswell himself. On June 20, 1771, when Boswell was still relatively prelapsarian, Johnson could find grounds as yet for guarded congratulation, but he hedged that about with apprehensive good counsel:

> I never was so much pleased as now with your account of yourself; and sincerely hope, that between publick business, improving studies, and domestick pleasures, neither melancholy nor caprice will find any place for entrance. . . . My dear Sir, mind your studies, mind your business, make your lady happy, and be a good Christian.

By 1779, replying to one of Boswell's *"black dog"* letters from Scotland, Johnson is showing a firmly established impatience:

> . . . I wish you to get rid of all intellectual excesses, and neither to exalt your pleasures, nor aggravate your vexations, beyond their real and natural state. Why should you not be as happy at Edinburgh as at Chester? *In culpa est animus, qui se non effugit usquam.* Please yourself with your wife and children, and studies, and practice.

By the summer of 1782 things were definitely going to pieces. Following the death of his father, Boswell wrote of his desire to come to London for Johnson's advice but complaining that his economy was in such a bad way that he could not afford the trip; to this Johnson's reply is abrupt and for the first time almost wholly without kindness:

> I am sorry to find, what your solicitation seems to imply, that you have already gone the whole length of your credit. This is to set the quiet of your whole life at hazard. . . . Live on what you have; live if you can on less; do not borrow either for vanity or pleasure; the vanity will end in shame, and the pleasure in regret: stay therefore at home, till you have saved money for your journey hither.

A recurrent theme in these later letters is admonition to Boswell to value and guard his wife, whose importance to him Johnson understood better than did Boswell himself: "I hope that dear Mrs. Boswell will surmount her complaints; in losing her you would lose your anchor, and be tost, without stability, by the waves of life." Upon this passage Boswell added, years later, a blubbering footnote, "The Truth of this has been proved by sad experience." As he nears his own end, Johnson's tone grows more and more acid:

> Like all other men who have great friends, you begin to feel the pangs of neglected merit; and all the comfort that I can give you is, by telling you that you have probably more pangs to feel, and more neglect to suffer. You have, indeed, begun to complain too soon; and I hope I am the only confidant of your discontent. . . . Of the exaltations and depressions of your mind you delight to talk, and I hate to hear. Drive all such fancies from you.

Still, it is very pleasant to find that two of his last letters, written in the summer before his death, while they continue to reprimand, also decisively return the balance toward kindness. Thus,

> Write to me often, and write like a man. I consider your fidelity and tenderness as a great part of the comforts which are left me, and sincerely wish we could be nearer to each other. . . . Love me as well as you can.

> Go steadily forward with lawful business or honest diversion. . . . This may seem but an ill return for your tenderness; but I mean it well, for I love you with great ardour and sincerity.

The rest of the story is famous and sad. Half of James Boswell died with Samuel Johnson in 1784 and the other half died with Margaret Montgomerie Boswell in 1789. Boswell had a way of falling into halves. What reeled on to 1795 was the husk of a man. Lord Auchinleck pressed the life from his son and when he had hollowed him out sent him into the world to be filled and propped, chemically, by alcohol and, psychologically, by men and women who had strength to spare. "I am quite restored by him," Boswell said of Johnson to Mrs. Thrale, "by transfusion of Mind." After the death of his wife he wrote to Temple, "I am the most helpless of human beings." Edmund Malone propped the husk long enough for it to patch together, with the shreds of its genius, one of the world's great books. "Let me not *think* at present," he wrote to Temple during that process; "far less *resolve*. The *Life of Johnson* still keeps me up. I *must* bring that forth, and then I think I may bury myself in London, in total obscure indifference. . . ." But the husk staggered back to Scotland and got itself buried there at last, after a course of events really too painful to record.

"You are longer a boy than others," Johnson told him. Old Auchinleck gave him his congenital wound: by refusing to let him be a boy when he was young he made him a boy when he was old. The boy of thirty-five who could write, "I must really get Mr. Johnson to put me down a short, clear system of Religion," could never grow up.

Whatever shame is due Boswell for his part in the life of Boswell, very little shame is due him for his part in the life of Johnson. The self of Boswell that served Johnson served him magnificently. Johnson required him to be a superb companion, and Boswell responded with a superb performance. "I believe Mr. Boswell will be at last your best Physician," Mrs. Thrale wrote Johnson in 1773—when he thought he was going mad. Reynolds writing to Langton of Boswell in 1782 quoted Burke's opinion: ". . . he is by much the most agreeable man he ever saw in his life." Johnson thought so too. It seems to me foolish and sentimental to overpraise Boswell. As the Compleat Son he was a heartbreaking, vicious failure. But as gay, vivid, articulate companion of the bosom, he justified Johnson in saying, as he did say, " 'I do love thee. I do love thee.' "

Justice to *Pamela*

"Well, my story, surely, would furnish out a surprising
kind of novel, if well told."   *—Pamela*

FTER staggering for years under a weight of
fame greater than he should ever have been
asked to support, Samuel Richardson fell, it
seems, and for a long time now he has lain
kicking feebly in the dust of literary history. His novels, great
in size and in some of their achievements, have joined that
honorable list of virtually unvisited monuments of English
fiction that includes, unhappily, *Bleak House*, *Middlemarch*,
Moby Dick, *The Marble Faun*, *The Wings of the Dove*,
and *Finnegans Wake*. Their wing of the museum has faithful
attendants but few paid admissions: it is kept open by subsidy.
Outside, in the open air of literary give and take, those few
cubits that are spent on Richardson's *Pamela* are full of cloudy
nonsense. I should like to lament that state of things and do
what I can to change it. I speak to those critics and historians
who depreciate *Pamela* because they misread it, and to the
schoolboy who has accepted too gratefully the judgment of
his tutors that *Pamela* is another important book that he need
not read. What I hope to do is to draw up a defense against
the two commonest and most serious indictments of the novel:
that it is fatally sentimental and artificial, and that its pretentious moralism is vicious and false. Literary judgments are
happily subjective, of course—that is why they are so much
fun and why people keep making them. But it is also why
opinions are likely to differ so widely, and why, when the
difference is diametrical, they tend to degenerate into childish

" 'Tis-'Tain't" squabbles. Such an ungraceful posture we may not be able to avoid here, but we can at least air and dramatize the vital point: that the Richardson issue is alive not dead.

My notion that *Pamela* is a novel of striking verisimilitude is by no means wholly heterodox, yet I think that emphasis in the received opinion, the schoolboy's mist, runs largely the other way. This seems to be a kind of standard schematic line of literary historians: Richardson is progenitor of the sentimental novel, not the realistic novel; he is a captive of Puritan theology, hence a slave to all the special pleading and distortion of view that that dogma enjoins; he is a creature circumscribed by the paraphernalia of middle-class sensibility— a shopkeeper with a shopkeeper's ethics and a shopkeeper's aesthetics; Richardson had to be satirized before we would have realism: the realistic tradition in the English novel begins with Fielding and *Joseph Andrews*, an avowed satire on *Pamela*. Thus Professor Cazamian leads off his chapter on "The Novel of Sentiment": ". . . Richardson, seeking his inspiration in Puritan sentimentalism. He has hardly written ere realism . . . sets up against his example an example that is openly contradictory. . . ."

Actually the scheme seems to me substantially if coarsely accurate; so my quarrel here is a gentle one, not with the substance of the historians' line but with its crudity. The historian does *Pamela* very serious injustice if he encourages the schoolboy to tick the novel off as *merely* sententious, sentimental, tiresomely moralistic, stiffly artifical, and hopelessly prolix (and so, obviously unreadable). There is truth in all these epithets, but still they do not contain Pamela, or explain her. Her story, I insist, is funny, it is touching, it is endlessly interesting, and beyond all these it is finally convincing: it grows true and actual. In spite of all its confessed vices, the novel does possess a dense and considerable verisimilitude. That is really all I want to argue at this point—that *Pamela* has a kind of residual realism that is much larger and more conclusive than critics like to admit: that it is a credible incredibility, a real unreality.

There is much that is patently unreal in *Pamela*, and we should begin by noticing its worst sins of falseness to life. These occur mainly in habits of style and of characterization. Thus the high rhetorical polish of the novel's utterance, its glossy surface and its elegant periodic undulation of syntactical movement—both beautiful and dull—is completely incredible as the epistolary style of a fifteen-year-old country girl. No servant girl, and no fifteen-year-old miss of any station, ever talked like this. I do not refer to her flux or her redundancy—which seem to me functional, charming and believable—but to her vocabulary, her range of reference, and her sentence structure, the general hand-rubbed finish of the discourse. Her rhetoric is superb, but in terms of character it is also absurd. The book is one long unbroken example of what I mean, and it is not even necessary to quote to prove the point.

Richardson's characterization, or rather his caricaturing of character, is a still more nagging flaw in his realism. Pamela, if we look at her only as she functions in the novel's tiresome moral line, is one-dimensional to paper-thinness; she is madly Puritanical, really a maniac of virtue. In a different direction Mrs. Jewkes and Lady Davers are also caricatures, character-absolutes of much crudeness in the conception, though undeniably, too, of an almost Dickensian gusto and impetus. Mr. B., while he is at least conventionally satisfactory as the baffled rake, is in no way convincing as the complacent husband—"palpably uxorious" was Milton's resonant phrase in another context for such behavior:

> . . . let me tell my sweet girl, that, after having been long tossed by the boisterous winds of a more culpable passion, I have now conquered it, and am not so much the victim of your beauty, all charming as you are, as of your virtue: and therefore may more boldly promise for myself, having so stable a founda-

tion for my affection, which, should this outward beauty fail, will increase with your virtue, and shine forth the brighter, as that is more illustriously displayed by the augmented opportunities your future condition will afford you.

"O the dear charming man," burbles Pamela; but the reader sees too plainly that his outright transformation is shoddily motivated and ridiculously complete. His absurd *gravitas* and airs of old age at twenty-six make him not a legitimately-altered character but simply an unfamiliar man. Thus Wilbur Cross was surely right when he said there was in Richardson "a lingering on of one form of allegory." But again this seems to be but a crude truth, and while it will carry us through a hurried paraphrase, it will by no means carry us to the real boundaries of the novel.

We may try, surrounded by Richardson's imperfections, to classify the means by which he converts the complex unreality of his subject, his form, and his personages into a reality considerable enough to catch, hold, and delight our attention. In order not to repeat the allegorist's emphatic error, let us remember now that reality is not absolute, not one but many. We may call for aid from a canonized realist, Henry James, who thought more often and more wisely about the art of the novel than anyone else. In "The Art of Fiction" James said:

> The characters, the situation, which strike one as real will be those that touch and interest one most, but the measure of reality is very difficult to fix. The reality of Don Quixote or of Mr. Micawber is a very delicate shade. . . .

In the same essay James testified to the importance of the issue:

> . . . the air of reality (solidity of specification) seems to me to be the supreme virtue of a novel—the merit on which all its other merits . . . helplessly and submissively depend. If it be not there they are all as nothing, and if these be there, they

owe their effect to the success with which the author has produced the illusion of life.

Reality is multiform and vital, and we are right to be interested in what Richardson *makes* us believe.

We see at once that *Pamela*'s persuasiveness is partly a matter of form and structure. In a purely technical sense, realism aside, the novel's worst vices are probably those of dramatic structure: it is too long for its essential work; too inclusive, too unselective; too often static in movement and slack in tension ("I like those great still books," Tennyson said, and wished for a novel of hundreds of volumes); it reaches its turning point much too early, proportionately, and the falling action is thus far too long and too merely thin and sweet. But if its sins are in part those of structure, so are its virtues. At the simplest level, we feel that the epistolary method itself carries a kind of gratuitous *cachet* of realism. That is, letters are normally vehicles for our common factual doings, a letter pre-supposes an actual writer and an actual reader, a letter is stiff and undramatic: if one wants to propound a fiction not a truth, why not choose a suppler, more active form? Our prior notions of the normal function of the form subtly if shallowly suggest to us an actual maiden, an actual seducer, and an actual marriage. The effect grows thicker as Richardson manipulates the epistles, the whole familiar machinery of hidden pens and ink and paper and wafers, of evasions and discoveries, of hidings in bosoms and underlinens and sunflowers. Then there is the whole clustering, hovering, lingering effect—later much multiplied in *Clarissa*—which comes to surround an incident as it goes its echoic progress in this method: the incident occurs, it is reflected on, committed to paper, committed to a porter, spied upon, received, reflected on, responded to, and perhaps returned to the original actors. The whole complex repercussive effect grows much thicker than the printed page. The epistolary form, too, excuses logically, though it does not justify artistically, much of the buttery smoothness of Pamela's unctuous rhetoric: that is, a letter is an editing of life, not life itself, and has an editor's option to tailor and furbish experience. So Richardson, having once posited a servant maid with flair and flow, can sensibly ask of us some suspension of disbelief—though by no means so full a suspension as he does in fact demand. As one quick instance of the conviction carried so simply by the epistolary form itself, consider the novel's first letter. There the cold plunge *in medias res* with the bald announcement of the death of old Lady B. and the immediate joining of the issue with her son have all the disorderly naïveté of life itself; it is only by hindsight that we see much later that they have as well all the ordered craft of art itself.

One does not know exactly how much verisimilitude to claim for Richardson's handling of the sequence of incident in *Pamela*. It is obvious in the first place that Richardson, in his somewhat fussy feminine way, is endlessly inventive of incident; but his inventiveness is not our present concern. More relevant is the fact that incidents in *Pamela* are likely to be little more than interesting fits of manners: if they are dramatic at all they are so in terms of revelation of personality rather than of deeps of character or morals. Still it seems to me that this admitted manneristic shallowness, while it disappoints our hopes of larger dramatic tension and thematic sweep, should not seriously disappoint our sense of drawing-room and boudoir reality, our humble guesses as to how life is normally conducted in such precious stations as the country-house environment of Mr. B. We should note as well in Richardson's favor that he depends very little—much less than the satire of *Joseph Andrews* implies—on pure coincidence or lucky accident in managing the sequence of incident: the confusing of Mr. B.'s letter to Mrs. Jewkes with that to Pamela is almost the only case that springs to mind. What is very damaging to the book's realism, on the other hand, is the stylized balancing of situations: outrage in the summer house is succeeded by sweet repentance in the summer house; tearful farewells by triumphant reunions; vulgar assertiveness by contrite capitulation. All this is much too meagre, pat, unmotivated—too sentimental, in a word.

But offsetting this distinctively wooden and artificial patterning of events Richardson offers two additional virtues of structure—a different order of repetition, and a large and noble quality we can best call modulation. This other simpler repetition is incremental, and it seems to me quietly hilarious. Instances of it are the superlative-plus-"in England" phrase pattern Richardson is so fond of—bluff, hearty and in its mingled dullness and good humor wonderfully life-like: "the loveliest girl in England," "the happiest man in England," "the honestest fellow in England." Or consider Richardson's exquisite fooling with the name of "Miss Sally Godfrey," with Pamela's fixation on that name like a mannerly lady bulldog once Lady Davers has rashly pronounced it, until the well-bred tension is all nicely relaxed with Mr. B.'s manly narrative of the days when he was a very bad boy indeed and his revelation of the sweet consequences of his error in little Miss Goodwin of the "fine black eye" and "genteel shape." All utterly phoney, yet still irresistibly affecting and, moreover, acceptable for the long moment of our reading as purest truth. Best of all in this line is Mr. B.'s fanatic urge to get his hand into Miss Andrews' cloistered bosom, where he infallibly blunders on the trigger that sets off her heroic serial fainting fits. The double fetishism of the maneuver is high low comedy, and especially in its testimony to masculine single-mindedness it is uproarious and real.

Now in all of this we may, if we choose, follow those readers who find Richardson humorless and helplessly moralistic: if we do so we have to call these and other repetitions nothing more than instances of slovenliness or sententiousness. But I think they are not so, and a careful reading of the management of tone and timing in the Sally Godfrey detail, especially, will show that they are conscious and delicious art. There is no question that they are delicious, the real question is whether or not they are conscious. If we were dealing with Fielding or Sterne or Smollett we would know where we are: with these writers a comic device is a comic device and announces itself distinctly in tonic incongruity. In the case of Richardson the facts are harder to come at. Biographical data are sadly scanty and inconclusive; lovable enough in his private posture as a man of family and of business, he is very hard to like at all in what we can see of his public postures as moralist and man of letters. There, in what we can gather from the fragmentary lives and the published correspondence, he stands forth as a limited, pompous man, more than a little silly in his costume of sage, and marked more than anything else by a drab and invulnerable sobriety—a little Hudibras. By no possible strain can we adduce humor to his statements about *Pamela*, of which the original full title of the work can be taken as an entirely fair sample:

> *Pamela: or, Virtue Rewarded.* In a series of Familiar Letters from a beautiful Young Damsel to her Parents. Now first published in order to cultivate the Principles of Virtue and Religion in the Minds of the Youth of both Sexes. A Narrative which has its Foundation in TRUTH and NATURE; and at the same time that it agreeably entertains, by a variety of curious and affecting INCIDENTS, is entirely divested of all those Images, which, in too many Pieces calculated for Amusement only, tend to inflame the Minds they should instruct.

Yet, conclusive as all this seems, I am sure it does not conclude. Richardson did have a comic sense: it was potentially fine, as the Howe-Hickman relationship in *Clarissa* shows. But his self-conscious moralism told him constantly to depress it, and it almost seems that it emerges in the novels only when it escaped him in moments of inattention on the part of his censorious conscience. All this is an instance, I think, of the curious fact to which we shall have to return: Richardson is a classic example of a man misreading himself. He thought he was a great moralist serving his texts in a merely adequate bolus of fiction; he was in fact a jejune moralist (not, I shall argue, a dishonest one) but a grand shaggy artist who was prevented by his own moral fatuity and that of his readers from ever seeing himself in an adequate mirror, currying his coat, and emerging as the truly first-rate novelist he should have been. In short, it seems to me we have to deal with a prime case of *unconscious* genius. The little tricks I have been mentioning above are minor manifestations of that fact.

That other softening quality I have called modulation is one not easy to demonstrate, since it is a property of the book's larger rhythms and makes itself felt almost unconsciously in the main. By modulation I mean here the achievement of topography and texture that is various and interesting—rise and fall, shading, ranges of mood and coloration, tension and release; the whole vague but vital matter of subjective flexibility within the objective strait-jacket of the epistolary form and the sentimentality of the theme. My point is that this variety, this orderly disorder, is the rhythm of life itself and that Richardson commands it skillfully in *Pamela*. Perhaps the best instance is his beautiful control of the slow, faltering, settling movement of Pamela's descent from the peak of her apprehension to the quiet confidence of the moment when Mr. B. indeed marries her in an invincibly legal ceremony in an unquestionable chapel furnished with an indisputable clergyman. Other cases are the nicely imagined (and startlingly modern) ambivalent pattern of Pamela's love-hate response to Mr. B. before the marriage, the slow conversion of Lady Davers, the fearful, delightful reaction of Goodman Andrews to the spectacle of his daughter's good fortune, the broadening and lightening of the comic tone on the two occasions when the seducer is driven to hiding in the sacred boudoir. Only three important elements in the novel seem to me totally lacking in this quality of modulation. One is the character of the married Mr. B., in which the absence of shading is a fundamental and very damaging flaw; another is Pamela's love for her parents, and one neither expects nor wants that to vary; the third is her redundant piousness: of her piety one cannot quite say that it is incredible—only that it is dreadfully dull.

After confessing above that the basic principle of characterization in *Pamela* approaches the allegorical, I suggested that that did not complete the matter. There is a strong residual reality in Richardson's persons that notably fleshes out the leanness of allegory. The heroine herself, who begins by being the most fully allegorical figure, ends by becoming the most fully human. Beginning in ignorance, one hopes for a time that Pamela is going to be a satirical figure: as such she would be quite perfect. But then one concludes, sadly at first, that Richardson has no satirical intention at all: he wants us to accept Pamela exactly as she fatally is, in full crushing sobriety—an impregnably Good Girl. This is disappointing, especially if one has trained on Fielding. But the thing that interests me now is how Richardson converts one, first, to acceptance of his whole sentimental convention and, next, to acceptance of the reality of this absurd little person and ultimately to delighted enlistment in the tension and truth of her maiden dilemma. He manages this, it seems to me, in a number of clear and legitimate ways: by setting her in a crux which, however much he chooses to cloy it, is inherently genuine and apposite to her way of life; by furnishing her with neatly counterpoised troops of friends and foes; by boning her fragility with an impressive willowy toughness and so making the balance reside in her own able little armory of innate powers, her craft and her ethics, her fanatical ability to cope—always a credible middle-class engine; by the pathos of the spectacle of the helpless old parents, quaking somewhere in the dim hinterland, hanging on with palpitations from letter to letter.

But still more interestingly Richardson satisfies our wish

for satire and our sense of the motley truth of human personality by making Pamela, in little ways that can do her no basic harm, a figure of fun. The obvious traits in this line are her prolixity, her fondness for dull particularity, her transparent rationalizations (". . . he had this moment sent me five guineas, by Mrs. Jervis, as a present for my pocket; so I shall be very rich; for as *she* brought them, I thought I might take them"); her disingenuous vanity (" 'Alas, Sir,' said I, my master coming up, 'mine is but a borrowed shine, like that of the moon. Here is the sun, to whose fervent glow of generosity I owe all the faint lustre that your goodness is pleased to look upon with so much kind distinction' "). And while equipping her with these harmless vices Richardson supplies her as well with considerable insight into them—that is, with self-knowledge. She knows that she is windy, and that it is part of her charm; she knows that she can be tiresomely circumstantial, that she is prone to construe motives to her own advantage, that she has a prehensile ear for praise. Our knowledge of her knowledge makes her immensely more tangible to our credence. Surely, for an allegorical figure, this is a creature strikingly rich; and, for one supposedly anemic, amusingly full of blood. Pamela must be the liveliest incarnation of chastity ever made. She is its abstract embodiment but she is also thoroughly concrete—fully clothed in bright and fluent particularity.

In further testimony to the realistic aspects of Richardson's characterization we should cite his handling of the brother-sister relationship between Mr. B. and Lady Davers. Considered singly, each is a type figure if not a purely allegorical one—though Lady Davers is a good deal more convincing as a human being than her brother. In spite of their individual stiffness, however, their behavior in their special office as siblings is perfectly life-like and very vivid as Richardson manages them. Their interaction is colored by a complex ambiguity that is both affecting and comic, and is beautifully functional in the novel's plot tissue. I am thinking now mainly of the way in which the physical and emotional maturity of the two is conditioned and complicated by an interesting remnant childishness, by strong passions inherent, first, in the nature of each, but aggravated and set in violent motion by the multiplied facts of their past relationship together as children—their mingled recollection of past trauma and past felicity, the insight of each into his own foibles and those of his fellow, the impetuousness, stubbornness, and headlong arrogance which they wear like a family livery and which they recognize, fear, despise, and finally forgive in each other. All of this is enriched by the purest kind of fraternal affection and respect that is not sentimental at all, and all of it, it seems to me, is deeply imagined and finely done by Richardson: it is one of the best things in the book, and one of the truest.

Perhaps we can review most of the remaining virtues of Richardson's realism under the heading of solidity: here again I borrow a phrase from Henry James's classic essay, where "solidity of specification" is his parenthetical equivalent for "the air of reality"—which we remember was for James "the supreme virtue of a novel." By solidity James meant that effect of depth and thickness which enjoins belief, and he felt this effect was mainly to be achieved by fullness and aptness of circumstantial detail. Now whatever else *Pamela* has or has not, it has solidity. Its solidity is in important part a matter of simple accumulation and artful selection of detail—every incident, every shift of manner or motive, abundantly furnished with data for the five senses to convince us of its actuality by reason of its situation in time and space and specific environment. Of many possible illustrations we may note just a few. How real and how focal become those first four fatal guineas: "I send them by John our footman, who goes your way: but he does not know what he carries, because I seal them up in one of the little pill-boxes, which my lady had, wrapped close in paper, that they mayn't chink; and be sure don't open it before him." How additionally palpable and comic for his costume is the seducer from the closet: ". . . O dreadful! out rushed my master in a rich silk and silver morning gown." Consider the verisimilitude of a single detail as Pamela squeezes through the bars of her boudoir prison, ". . . not without some difficulty, sticking a little at my hips." How lively and vivid is the flashing vignette of those three relics of Mr. B.'s unregenerate youth when they come to call on him as stately Benedict: ". . . three mad rakes they seemed to be, setting up a hunting note, as soon as they came to the gate, that made the court-yard echo again: and smacking their whips in concert." Or consider the abundant factuality of those three enlightening catalogs, Mr. B.'s "naughty articles," as Pamela calls them, her recitative of her proposed regimen as country wife, and the forty-eight points of her gloss from her husband's "awful lecture."

But let us join the moral issue at last. It is a knottier question than that of Richardson's realism, but the question is single and we may be able to satisfy it in a briefer exegesis. The problem begins, I suppose, with the novel's subtitle, "Virtue Rewarded," and what seems its clear double premise —that virtue must receive a tangible recompense, and that one practises virtue *in order* to receive this recompense. An unbroken long line of critics have found the cash-register morality implied in the subtitle fulfilled in the tissues of the novel, and have roundly damned Richardson therefor. It is this condemnation, which I find wrong-headed and over-emphatic, which appears to have done most of the heavy lifting in the casting of Richardson into outer darkness. It is Pamela's innocent parents who, in the novel's second letter, incautiously provide the metaphor that has seemed to satisfy the figurative demands of generations of critics: do not, they warn her, "reward him with that jewel, your virtue." Monotonously through the years the critics have rung the weary changes on that figure and on Pamela the artful enginer, the virtue-vendor, the good-girl-with-a-purpose. From the last fifty years or so we might cite Mrs. Thomson, Leslie Stephen, Austin Dobson, and Joseph Wood Krutch. But Mr. Krutch is the most recent and much the most trenchant and we can depend on him to state the normal indictment without mumbling. I quote the crucial paragraphs on *Pamela* from his beautiful long essay in *Five Masters*:

> Nor is it possible, as one follows with amazement the proud exposition of her principles, to discover in them anything except the logical development of a shrewd determination to get as much as possible out of the world, for if we judge her by the evidence of her own letters she is a prig at best and a designing minx besides. Richardson had set out to describe his ideal of feminine character but he had created instead a coarse-minded opportunist because he had himself achieved a cynicism more complete than is possible to any except those unaware of their own principles. The virtue of Pamela is no more than a realization of the fact that her virginity is by far the most valuable of her possessions and a wise determination not to lose what has a perfectly tangible value. . . .

> Yet it is possible to account for every detail of her behaviour without any reference whatsoever to any principle belonging in the realm of morals. Like all maidens she had a jewel and the precious possession was one to be safeguarded with all the watchfulness of a traveller who passes through some bandit-infested waste. The thing—though to all appearances no more than a pretty trifle—has a value, thanks to which it can be bartered or sold, and therefore it must not be lost. He who allows it to be taken from him is criminally careless; he who gives it away is a fool. . . . Skill in trade is a citizen's virtue. Pamela held out for a good price and in the end she got it. Thus is virtue rewarded.

All this is clear enough, surely. I react to it with a variety of emotions, chiefly amazement and a kind of detached rage. I simply cannot see it: there is no real evidence for such a view of *Pamela*. May I, humbly, well knowing Mr. Krutch's range and acumen as a critic, submit that in this instance he is guilty

of a serious misreading, at the very least of an exaggeration
equal to falsification. His statement is finely emphatic but it
seems to me simply untrue. I am reminded here of Richardson's complaint against *Joseph Andrews* as a "lewd and ungenerous engraftment" upon *Pamela*. Taking Mr. Krutch's
diagnosis as an eloquent norm of the standard indictment of
the novel's morality, and hoping not to echo Richardson's
accent of adolescent aggrievement, I should say that such
analyses are lewd in attributing to the heroine a prurience and
a crassness which are simply not discoverable in the text; ungenerous in refusing to grant the true harshness of her em-
pirical situation; an engraftment in applying a moral criterion that is in some sense anachronistic and impertinent. Pamela
needs to be handled without mawkishness but with more
charity and more common sense. But this gets us nowhere
until we examine the text.

Let us face the facts of life for Pamela. She is fifteen
years old, the daughter of "poor but honest" parents—that
ghastly phrase—who have descended, through excessive faith
in man, from modest competence and gentility to impover-
ished peasanthood. Providence has given her extraordinary
beauty, charm, and presence; her good old mistress has taught
her social graces (and a few airs) far more sophisticated than
her origins; her parents have taught her the limited Protestant
morality of their time and station. Of this world's goods she
possesses, almost literally, nothing. She does possess the divine
benefice of every otherwise naked human being, her virtue,
which naturally (since society never ceased pointing at it so
crudely) came to center in its physical embodiment in the
fragile little membrane which is its seal and symbol. *Of
course* it has value—value first as emblematic of purity, and
value in the countenance of the world (and of the church)
as a generic commodity, the only one she owns. Now how
does Pamela treat her emblem? How much evidence can we
find in the text of the novel for Mr. Krutch's character of

her as a "designing minx," a "coarse-minded opportunist," a "dealer in precious stones" whose virtue is the "citizen's virtue" of the crafty bargainer?

From the moment when Mr. B. first "offers freedoms" and Pamela sounds the tocsin of beleaguered innocence, she is packed, ready, and eager to flee back to her "little bed in the loft." Nothing in her tone or her actions, it seems to me, can allow one legitimately to question the depth or the sincerity of her repeated protestations to that effect. He resolves to send her home and she thanks him on her knees, and writes her parents, "And thus all is happily over." Looking ahead to her return to poverty, she writes, ". . . I hope to make my hands as red as a blood pudding, and as hard as a beechen trencher to accommodate them to my condition." She vacillates momentarily when it looks as if she may be allowed to remain with honor to herself and benefit to her parents, then when it becomes clear that honor is not in it she is again all adamant resolution to be gone. She plots with Mr. Williams elaborate escapes, then when those are undermined she makes a genuinely perilous attempt alone. She resists a real temptation to suicide. Her resolve through all of this is solid and undissembled and so, it seems to me, is its moral base. Her resolution begins to waver, clearly, only with the wavering of her antagonist's deviltry. When the spectacle of her impregnability and the persuasiveness of her prose have begun to soften and sweeten and cleanse him, when it begins to seem that he may think of her humbly as his wife rather than arrogantly as his harlot, then indeed Pamela softens, too, recognizing with surprise her submerged regard for him. But her reaction is slow, timorous, embarrassed; there is none of the delighted gloat of the triumphant schemer, none of the rehearsed response of the woman who knew it all the time. And when Mr. B. turns furiously once more and sends her away, she goes still honestly and willingly, though slowly and sadly now, regretting what might have been:

46

I think I was loth to leave the house. Can you believe it? —
What could be the matter with me, I wonder? I felt something
so strange and my heart was so lumpish! I wonder what ailed
me! But this was so *unexpected*!—I believe that was all. Yet I
am very strange still. Surely, I cannot be like the old murmur-
ing Israelites, to long after the onions and garlic of Egypt,
when they had suffered there such heavy bondage?—I'll take
thee, O lumpish, contradictory, ungovernable heart, to severe
task, for this thy strange impulse, when I get to my dear father's and mother's; and if I find anything in thee that should
not be, depend upon it, thou shalt be humbled, if strict absti-
nence, prayer, and mortification will do it.

There is no crassness in any of this and no vulgarity. The
morality with which Richardson equips Pamela is not complicated, not rich, not of itself very interesting: we may legitimately find it dull. We may not, on the other hand, legitimately find it contemptible or corrupt.

The viciousness of Pamela's morality, her detractors may
say, is implicit rather than explicit—between the lines of the
text rather than in them. This view would have it that while
Pamela persuades the world that she is frantically defending
her virtue she is in fact, under cover of the hurly-burly, conducting a subtle and rotten campaign against the heart and
especially the estate of Mr. B.: her virtue is not her besieged
bastion but her sally-port. But to read this in the story is to
find there more than Richardson either stated or implied. If
we examine the charges in this line, that, for example, Pamela
dresses out her charming "person" to be seductive to Mr. B.,
we find them overstrained. Mr. B. cannot be blamed for
being taken with such a fetching image, we must agree:

. . . I dressed myself in my new garb, and put on my round-
eared ordinary cap, but with a green knot, my home-spun gown
and petticoat, and plain leather shoes, but they are what they
call Spanish leather; and my ordinary hose, ordinary I mean to
what I have been lately used to, though I should think good
yarn may do very well for every day, when I come home. A
plain muslin tucker I put on, and my black silk necklace, in-

stead of the French necklace my lady gave me; and put the ear-
rings out of my ears. When I was quite equipped, I took my
straw hat in my hand, with its two blue strings, and looked in
the glass, as proud as anything. To say the truth, I never liked
myself so well in my life.

But neither can Pamela be charged with making herself
consciously seductive. She assembled the costume as one appropriate to her willing return to humble life; she put aside much
richer clothes as inappropriate; she put on the new simple
costume for Mrs. Jervis' approval; Mr. B. sees her in it
by chance, not by her design. Every comparable instance
which may be charged with a disingenuous motive may be
more strongly defended as possessing an entirely ingenuous
motive.

Pamela is so very far from conniving to ensnare Mr. B.
that she is completely, and completely honestly, amazed when
the thing indeed occurs. I think we cannot refuse to believe
exactly what Richardson wants us to believe: that the event
is the doing not of her art but of her morality and her "parts"
—her beauty, her good sense, her delightful overmastering
literacy. I do not mean that Richardson fails to prepare us for
the idea that Pamela is unconsciously in love with Mr. B. or
that she will have him when he offers honestly; quite the
contrary is true, he prepares us carefully and very well. The
preparation begins with that little generalizing penetration of
Pamela's in an early letter, "Is it not strange, that love borders so much upon hate?", and continues through a long sequence of such quiet signal statements until the eventual
reformation, proposal, acceptance, and felicity. Pamela's behavior throughout is consistent, logical, and respectable. She
is right to rebuff Mr. B., right to fail to hate him, and right
to accept him at last.

But if Pamela's actions are theoretically or ideally de-
fensible, if hers is the right way to behave to a good man,
should she behave as she does to *this* man? There indeed is

the crux. It is easily possible to say sourly with Mr. Krutch
and others that Richardson "had rewarded virtue by giving
it the hand of a rake"—hence, obviously, that that virtue
which receives a tainted reward must have been a tainted
virtue. When I say at last that Pamela should not have accepted Mr. B. I intend no captious paradox. The point that
needs to be made about all this is one that writers on Richardson persistently overlook: the failure involved in Pamela's
acceptance of Mr. B. is not a moral hiatus but an *artistic* one.
I mean that Pamela is made to respond nobly to an ignoble
stimulus: the fault is not in the response but in the stimulus.
Our outrage should not be so much moral as psychological.
What is involved is simple inadequacy in character drawing.
When Richardson wrote *Pamela* he was not conscious or
practised enough artistically, or sufficiently knowledgeable of
masculine psychology, to be able to make Mr. B. complicated
or flexible or full-blooded enough to deserve the hand of his
heroine. He fails to deserve her not because he is evil but
because he is not alive. What offends us in this marriage-
dance is not the union of virtue and vice but the union of
woman and mannikin. This inadequacy is the novel's worst
crudeness, but the crudeness is in the art, not in the morality.
Later Richardson atoned for it in the much finer figure of
Lovelace in *Clarissa.*

Critics of Richardson's morality are in great danger of
committing Richardson's own sins of humorlessness and sentimentality. It is both humorless and sentimental, *i. e.,* un-
realistic, to demand of Pamela, as we seem to do, a morality
that is either absolute or very sophisticated. For where, in her
own personality, her fiscal position, her creator's mind, or the
atmosphere of the times, would she be expected to find it?
She was dirt-poor, her moral equipment was drawn from the
stupidest depositories of eighteenth-century Protestantism,
she was fixed in a menial position in the power of an arrogant
class which defined its menials as chattels and habitually used

them as such (was it not the stout Fielding himself who got his dead wife's nursemaid with child before he condescended to marry her?)—what would we have? She must make her way and make it naked and alone. Do we really want to send her back to her little bed in the loft? Even if we admit—as I insist the text does not force us to admit—that while Pamela rode the horse Good Girl she led the pony Good Marriage, how seriously and realistically can we complain? Or how *morally*?

> Most vertuous virgin! glory be thy meed,
> And crowne of heavenly prayse with saintes above. . . .

It may be that we need to borrow some of Richardson's own sturdy pragmatism in our view of the novel. I am thinking of such things as his clear-eyed confession of the reality of power and weakness; of the functionality of appearance— what beauty will buy; of the overwhelming importance of *things*—of clothes, for example, above all, of money. It may be said with some justice that money makes the real mood-music of this novel; it clinks and jingles unremittingly, just loud enough to hear, little golden bells on the trace-chains of the action. This is a novel about virtue hard beset, but it is also a novel about prosperity won by beauty, by wit, by ade-quacy to the event—and by virtue. I wonder if we need so violently to deplore the peasantish pragmatic substructure of *Pamela*, its bedrock of tough common sense. May we not assume, wistfully, that virtue and prosperity may coexist, with-out adducing therein a necessary causative relation? Whatever its disappointing simplicities, Richardson's moral dialectic never insists on that. What we have in this printer is the same thing we have in that other good journeyman, Ben Franklin. No, we have to say, finally, that the great fault in Richard-son's morality is not its corruptness but its conventionality. Angered with the ordinary man for not being a giant, we are calling him a pigmy. Expecting too much, we have been unreasonably insulting. Richardson's moral scheme is discouragingly thin, it is dull, it is much too simple, but it is not laughable at any point.

Richardson is not of the company of the "thought-divers," as Melville called them, the men with the "red eyes": that much is clear. But he is no joke, and I think it is time we stopped patronizing him. He is, as I have tried to argue, a shaggy amateur artist who should have been great, a man whose genius remained unfulfilled because it was unconscious. His originality is immense, and so, as everyone admits, is his historical service. The reader furnished with the historian's notion that *Pamela* is the first full novel in English comes at the book with a sense of shock and gratitude: if this is the first of its kind, then where, one asks, is its primitiveness? This is an invention of startling completeness: like Athene it seems to spring to life full-blown. One feels in reading it the same sensation, but larger and more intensified and of a higher order, that one feels in reading Poe's *Murders in the Rue Morgue*, where the first formal detective story emerges as the sufficient sire of all that were to come later. In both cases the invention is total and conclusive. It is certainly true that Fielding had to reform the solid but simple-minded morality of *Pamela*. And it is true that Fielding and others had to teach the novel niceties of structure—selection and proportion—and grace and economy of movement; but aside from that there was little that anybody needed to teach Richardson, technically, about the writing of a novel. He knew how it was done, and he knew how to keep the anesthetic of Puritan morality from immobilizing life. That is the very considerable artistic achievement of this novel. We need not condescend to it, but read it.

Utmost Merriment, Strictest Decency: *Joseph Andrews*

IELDING's "comic epic-poem in prose," *Joseph Andrews*, ends with the neat bow-knot effect that is habitual and right for English classical comedy, with the proper comic "catastrophe," a marriage. The hero, "drest . . . in a neat, but plain suit of Mr. Booby's, which exactly fitted him," leads Fanny dressed in "nothing richer than a white dimity nightgown" undergirded by a lace-edged shift and fine white thread stockings, presents from her sister Pamela, and simply crowned by "one of her own short round-ear'd caps, and over it a little straw hat, lined with cherry-coloured silk, and tied with a cherry-coloured ribbon," across the country turf to the church. There they are gravely married by their old friend and ghostly father Parson Abraham Adams, who interrupts the service to rebuke Pamela and Mr. Booby for laughing. After the ceremony the wedding company proceed on foot to Mr. Booby's house, where the day is passed "with the utmost merriment, corrected by the strictest decency," and enjoyed by none more gaily than by Parson Adams, "well filled with ale and pudding." At last Fanny is undressed for bed and joined by Joseph, who confirms that, as he has long suspected, "undressing to her was properly discovering, not putting off, ornaments: for, as all her charms were the gifts of nature, she could divest herself of none." It is a nice question to consider why all these details of the nuptials, so ordinary in themselves, are so very far from perfunctory as we experience them. The whole event seems chaste, plain, natural. But by the end of the tale simplicity has accumulated great richness. Motions have become motives; every gesture, every detail serenely bears a weight of meaning and feeling in the comic dance, grave and gay. The parts inherit the significance of the design which they have joined to compose.

Offended by the huge popular success of Richardson's *Pamela* in the fall and winter of 1740, Fielding hurriedly printed under a pseudonym his murderously ribald pamphlet-parody *Shamela* in the spring of 1741. Still amused and revolted by what he saw as the cash-register and social-register morality of *Pamela*, Fielding then commenced *Joseph Andrews* as a more elaborate and crushing satirical corrective. As one of the minority who *believe* Pamela throughout her serial assault and final triumph in capitulation, I feel some sympathy for Richardson's description of this second amendment as "a lewd and ungenerous engraftment." But that is an unfair and incomplete way to describe the book Fielding ultimately wrote. *Joseph Andrews* is a great work because it put aside its small and negative impulse and grew into a vehicle strong enough to carry Fielding's powers at full stretch.

The book begins parodically, or, in the terms of Fielding's preface, in the vein of "Caricatura" or "Burlesque," with that Pamela "whose virtue is at present so famous" installed as the distant presiding genius over the beleaguered chastity of her brother, footman to Lady Booby in London: ". . . it was by keeping the excellent pattern of his sister's virtues before his eyes, that Mr. Joseph Andrews was chiefly enabled to preserve his purity in the midst of such great temptations." In the good old way of parody, Fielding has simply upended the titillating situation of *Pamela*, presenting Joseph in the character of Male Virtue whose resolute and sententious purity turns the amorous Lady Booby into the " 'statue of Surprise' ": " 'Did ever mortal hear of a man's virtue!" she rages. " '. . . And can a boy, a stripling, have the confidence to talk of his virtue?' " " 'Madam,' " Joseph solemnly responds, " 'that boy is the brother of *Pamela*, and would be ashamed that the chastity of his family, which is preserved in her, should be stained in him.' " The mode of parody briefly extends itself, in two letters from Joseph to his sister, to outright imitation of Richardson's epistolary style. In fact, the parody virtually ends here, at the beginning. *Joseph Andrews* changes into something else under Fielding's hand. Richardson's novel, his heroine, and Fielding's specific animosity are in effect forgotten, and when Pamela and Mr. Booby reappear, briefly and delightfully, at the end of the action, they have been trimmed and reduced to fit a comic and moral design far larger than themselves. It is not quite accurate to say that the critique of *Pamela*, as understood and contemned by Fielding, has been abandoned. What ceases is the direct inverted satirical reference. The negative attack turns positive and changes shape and size. Fielding's critique finally takes the richest possible form, that of a wholly realized alternative morality, a new world fully conceived and dramatized, completing itself with marriage in the country parish. Once his own action is well begun Fielding really has no time for Samuel Richardson.

His action takes the ancient form of the journey, already classical in the eighteenth century. It is naturally a loose, episodic, horizontal form, but open to purpose and rhythm, and capable of infinite modulation. The journey as imagined by Fielding involves a physical progress and a secular quest, but as the long flex of the road is complicated by one significant experience after another, his journey thickens with moral meanings. The quest grows spiritual while remaining both dramatic and comic. It is a comic Pilgrim's Progress, concurrently reverent and gay: utmost merriment corrected by the strictest decency. The poles of the journey are the London mansion and the country church. Of course Joseph Andrews is not the only traveler. In his progress toward rural Somersetshire he is joined first by Parson Adams and then by Fanny.

54

They are overtaken by Lady Booby's lofty outriders, Mrs. Slipslop and Peter Pounce, and at last by the coach and six of the great lady herself; so that finally "the whole procession," as Fielding names it, descends upon Booby Hall to share in the instructive and entertaining episodes of the close.

Fielding organizes the journey toward that instruction and entertainment, imposes a graceful and light-reined control, by means of certain recurrent images and emphases that are best seen as metaphors, coordinating figures that indicate and compose a coherent design. The act of traveling itself and the various modes of movement become such a figure, for example: it matters morally from what, to what, and by what means one travels. Clothing and speech become metaphors; so do teaching and learning. The shape and carriage of the body has meaning. The uninsistent but persistent pattern of analogy, Biblical and classical, functions metaphorically. With great good humor, Fielding is assembling a comprehensive moral system, or more accurately a moral vision, on Christian principles.

The dominant motives begin to collect even as the narrative is still laboring to detach itself from the smaller sardonicism of its first impulse. We meet Joseph on the brink of his majority. Apprenticed at ten years on Sir Thomas Booby's country estate, he has been ennobled, by virtue of a combination of personal comeliness, trustworthiness, intrepid horsemanship, and sweetness of voice and temper, to be Lady Booby's favorite footman. She would like to promote him to her bed. He stands perilously poised in the wicked city, rustic *in urbe*. Lady Booby has already been heartened by "the effects which the town-air hath on the soberest constitutions." So far Joseph's corruption amounts only to a little harmless vanity. He is a natural prince of his kind. As on the farm he "constantly rode the most spirited and vicious horses to water," so in the city he "led the opinion of all the other footmen at the opera. . . ." He has begun to go about in the morning with his hair in papers. He is behaving less solemnly in church. In fact he is already "outwardly a pretty fellow," in the pejorative sense of that phrase. But he is still pure in heart, and, as his "party-coloured brethren"—in the phrase with which Fielding begins to associate clothing and character—have failed to teach him drinking and gambling, so Lady Booby fails to teach him adultery. He is defended, as he writes to Pamela, by his sister's noble example and by the godly instruction he has had in the country from Parson Adams. But "*London* is a bad place," as he says in his first letter, and he is not altogether sorry to be forced out of it.

Having resisted the advances not only of Lady Booby, "who had been bless'd with a town-education," but also of her waiting-gentlewoman Mrs. Slipslop, who "had been frequently at London," Joseph is "stript" of his livery, in the energetic word that is several times repeated, and cast off in the world. Like his great namesake, he has preserved his virtue by leaving his garment with Potiphar's wife: Joseph notes the analogy himself. His pilgrimage begins tentatively when he turns his back on London, puts "his best leg foremost," and sets off cross-country to the west and Somerset. London is a good place to leave, and the act of leaving is in part purgative and penitential: the stripping off of the livery partakes of that symbolism.

But the journey fully begins, as it must, twenty miles farther on, when he is beaten and left for dead in the ditch, stripped even of his borrowed livery, and reduced to a literal naked soul, the poor bare forked animal itself. The first dramatization ensues of one of Fielding's great running themes, the definition, in action, of Christian charity. The obvious analogue is the Parable of the Good Samaritan, though Fielding collects the serial travelers in a blatant mass, a coachman and his party of passengers, each of whom rejects the sufferer for his own selfish reasons. Again the whole brutal affair moves forward in the climate of robust comedy. The exces-

sively genteel lady, offended at the sight of a naked man, holds
the *sticks* of her fan before her eyes. The vulgarity of the
lawyer's speech announces the smallness of his mind and the
hardness of his heart:

> He said, "If *Joseph* and the lady were alone, he would be more
> capable of making a conveyance to her, as his *affairs* were not
> fettered with any *incumbrance*; he'd warrant he soon suffered
> a *recovery* by a writ of *entry*, which was the proper way to cre-
> ate *heirs in tail* . . .

and so on. Ultimately Joseph is relieved, in a way appropriate
to both fables, by the poor postillion, "a lad who hath been
since transported for robbing a hen-roost." The action cuts
another die for the novel, the upwelling of charity from the
poor and pure. In the next scenes, for example, the fountain
of charity flows not in the professional men of the village, the
surgeon and the clergymen, nor in the publicans of the
Dragon, Mr. and Mrs. Tow-wouse, but in the poor chambermaid Betty, whose amorousness seems a function of her inclusive generosity.

The local professional men pale and shrink in size when
Parson Adams enters the scene, with his formidable learning
and his formidable physical presence, his fist "rather less than
the knuckle of an ox," his wrist "which Hercules would not
have been ashamed of," and his heart in proportion. Adams,
one of the grand inventions of literature, raises the book to the
robustness of spirit which it sustains to the end. He happens
upon the Dragon on his way to London to sell nine volumes
of his sermons. Unluckily his downright spouse has filled his
saddlebags instead with shirts and "necessaries" for the journey. He accepts the mischance with perfect cheerfulness; it
points him for his home, his "cure," which is where he prefers
to be in any case: " 'No, child. . . . This disappointment may
perhaps be intended for my good.' " Adams' sublime forget-
fulness and absence of mind is an aspect of his comedy and a
device of plot; in the affair of the sermons, however, Fielding

wants it to suggest some of the meanings of the journey meta-phor. London is no place for Adams: he belongs, as he knows, with his "flock." His characteristic doctrine of good works, moreover, is scarcely portable or vendable: it is a matter of action and performance.

When in Book II Joseph and Parson Adams take up their way toward the country parish, the world lies all before them, full of opportunities for good works, Christian testing. In the little chapter prefatory to this book, Fielding brings even his amiable dialogue with the reader, cursive and discursive, into the service of his journey metaphor. He invites the reader to regard such an interchange as "an inn or resting-place, where he may stop and take a glass, or any other refreshment, as it pleases him"; and his chapter-headings as "so many inscriptions over the gates of inns . . . informing the reader what enter-tainment he is to expect, which if he likes not, he may travel on to the next. . . ." Having only one horse, an eccentric beast fond of kneeling, which Adams has borrowed from his clerk, Joseph and Adams resolve to "ride and tie," in the manner customary for two travelers with but one horse. Fielding ex-plains the method and goes on to moralize upon it.

> The two travellers set out together, one on horseback, the other on foot: now, as it generally happens that he on horseback out-goes him on foot, the custom is, that, when he arrives at the distance agreed on, he is to dismount, tie the horse to some gate, tree, post or other thing, and then proceed on foot; when the other comes up to the horse, he unties him, mounts, and gallops on, till, having passed by his fellow-traveller, he likewise ar-rives at the place of tying. And this is that method of travelling so much in use among our prudent ancestors, who knew that horses had mouths as well as legs, and that they could not use the latter without being at the expense of suffering the beasts themselves to use the former. This was the method in use in those days: when, instead of a coach and six, a member of par-liament's lady used to mount a pillion behind her husband; and a grave serjeant at law condescended to amble to Westminster on an easy pad, with his clerk kicking his heels behind him.

Fielding has here brought together the book's three modes of travel, those which Adams later names as "the pedestrian," "the equestrian," and "the vehicular." The coach and six, the eighteenth century's Rolls Royce, becomes one of the book's talismanic objects; but indeed all three modes become means to the drawings of moral distinctions.

Fielding's travels turn ramshackle at once. Adams, who has typically insisted on taking the first pedestrian stage, equally typically forgets to pay for his horse's keep at the inn, and Joseph is detained at the Dragon in that default, having unwisely revealed his possession of another talismanic object, his bit of gold tied with a ribbon, a keepsake from Fanny. Adams presses on, filling out the character designed by Fielding as "the most glaring in the whole." When he realizes that Joseph has been delayed he continues slowly forward, straight through a pond up to his middle because it does not occur to him to look over the hedge for a footpath. Then he composes himself upon a stile and pulls out his Aeschylus. The Book, too, is Fielding's talisman; not the Aeschylus only but books in general, the thing, the concept. Fielding has already announced that Adams is "designed a character of perfect simplicity." By simplicity he means innocence. Adams' inward absorption, which leads to his absence of mind, has nothing to do with egotism: it is never himself that he contemplates. He inhabits the real world in a state of wonderful nakedness, and strides through it as unconsciously as a Herculean baby. He possesses no practical rationalizing equipment through which to sift and edit the world, and so he reacts to experience with perfect spontaneity and primitive directness. His reactions tend to be otherwise abstract and disjunct from the case at hand, for he does possess a kind of irrelevant rationalizing mechanism, which he has derived from his learning. His learning is immense but it is wholly abstract, altogether an affair of books, and those spiritual and antique. He knows the classics, especially Homer, Aeschylus, and Aristotle, as he knows the scriptures, almost verbatim. For him the scriptures and the ancient pagans, as they are the whole of knowledge, constitute Truth. Thus the book is for Adams a sacred object, and "his Aeschylus" preeminently so—copied out by his own hand, bound in sheepskin, and lovingly conned for thirty years. Of the real world of men and their motives he is so perfectly unknowing that he lives in a state of chronic surprise, in alternate delight and rage. His ignorance of more modern learning is equally absolute. As he says, unblushingly, he is "not much travelled in the history of modern times, that is to say, these last thousand years." *Cato* is the only modern tragedy he has read, and he can think of no plays apart from *Cato* and *The Conscious Lovers* fit for a Christian to read.

Adams is finally overtaken by Joseph and the horse, ransomed by Mrs. Slipslop, who travels with a party of ladies roundly denounced by the coachman as "a parcel of squinnygut b--s." The pedestrian, the equestrian, and the vehicular modes are now joined again. An argument ensues as to which of the men is to occupy the empty seat in the coach. Amorous Slipslop prefers Joseph, but he "knows his duty better than to ride in a coach while Mr. Adams was on horseback," and one of the ladies refuses to ride with "a fellow in a livery," so Adams perforce ascends. One begins to see that Fielding is counterpointing a vertical figure against the running horizontal metaphor of the journey. The vertical metaphor is a social one, a ladder of power and privilege, actual or wishful, a principal embodiment of the great theme of vanity and affectation announced in the first prefatory chapter. The pedestrian, the equestrian, and the vehicular are stages on the social ladder. They also stand for degrees of intimacy with or detachment from the earth, the road, the great outflung horizontal image of the novel. Joseph and Parson Adams stay as close to the earth as they can. Their instinct is locomotor, to move their own bodies by an act of their own will: they know in their bones that their right movement is not upward but forward.

But now Adams is taken into the coach, as is Joseph later, long enough to provide an auditor from the central action for Fielding's extended aside, his digression formally entitled "The History of Leonora, or the Unfortunate Jilt." The tale itself is a moral fable, an exemplum on the dangers of vanity. Fielding emphasizes rather than obscures the artificiality of its insertion in the narrative fabric. He proceeds with something between a wink and a grin, as a part of his general joke with the reader, making use of a number of broad rhetorical devices. The formal title is one of these, as is the pointedly absurd transition into the tale:

> Thus Mr. Adams and she discoursed; 'till they came opposite to a great house which stood at some distance from the road; a lady in the coach spying it, cry'd "Yonder lives the unfortunate Leonora, if one can justly call a woman unfortunate whom we must own at the same time guilty and the author of her own calamity." This was abundantly sufficient to awaken the curiosity of Mr. Adams. . . .

The mincing elegance of the lady's narrative style conveys Fielding's scorn for the contemporary romance-writers, as does her "happening" to have by heart two lengthy letters of the lovers of her story. But serious meanings move always through the comedy in *Joseph Andrews*, and continuing means and motives are at work within this farce. Names matter, as always, and in "The Unfortunate Jilt" the effete Latinity of Leonora, Lindamira, Florella, and Bellarmine is set against the bluff solidity of Horatio. Bellarmine is not only citified but Parisian, urbane to the point of caricature. The greedy and frivolous Leonora is smitten first by Bellarmine's conveyance, a coach and six of course, which she declares to be "the completest, genteelest, prettiest equipage she ever saw," and to which she responds in a disastrously fundamental way: " 'O, I am in love with that equipage!' " Her conquest is completed, naturally, by Bellarmine's costume: ". . . a cut velvet coat of a cinnamon colour, lined with pink satin, embroidered all over with gold; his waistcoat, which was cloth of silver, was embroidered with gold likewise." When he singles her out at the ball, she knows the kind of triumph possible only to absolute vanity: "She had never tasted anything like this happiness. She had before known what it was to torment a single woman; but to be hated and secretly cursed by a whole assembly was a joy reserved for this blessed moment." To this sorry business Adams makes the response fundamental to his own nature, a series of deep groans.

The coaching party comes abreast of Joseph at an inn, recovering from the effects of a tumble with the genuflecting horse, pauses long enough for a combat in which Adams and his cassock receive a bath of hog's blood, and resumes its way with Joseph in the coach. Adams forgets the horse a second time, and, following his native preference for the pedestrian mode, "finding his legs as nimble as he desired," sets out in advance of the coach, brandishing his crabstick. When the coach approaches Adam thinks he is being challenged to a race and responds athletically.

> Mrs. *Slipslop* desired the coachman to overtake him, which he attempted, but in vain; for the faster he drove, the faster ran the parson, often crying out, "Ay, ay, catch me if you can," till at length the coachman swore he would as soon attempt to drive after a greyhound; and, giving the parson two or three hearty curses, he cry'd, "Softly, softly, boys," to his horses, which the civil beasts immediately obeyed.

Leaving the coach behind Adams comes to a point where, "by keeping the extremest track to the right, it was just barely possible for a human creature to miss his way," keeps the extremest track to the right, and misses his way. He communes with his Aeschylus for a time, then strikes out cross-country and arrives at that point in Christendom where Fanny Goodwill is about to be overcome by a ravisher. Fanny had got wind of Joseph's difficulties in London, and, with the full-blooded readiness of response natural to Fielding's pure in heart, had abandoned the cow she was milking, bundled up her clothes and her money, and set off on foot for the city to rescue the lover she acknowledges only to her inmost heart. With his crabstick and his fist rather less than the knuckle of an ox, Adams subdues the assailant, and, after one more brush with farcical forms of the law and the clergy, he and Fanny are free to join Joseph.

Fielding contrives the meeting at the next inn, making use of one of the ironically disjunct rhetorical patterns with which he likes to dress his climaxes. From a neighboring room Fanny and Adams hear a voice, "one of the most melodious that ever was heard," singing a saccharine pastoral lyric beginning, "Say, Chloe, where must the swain stray/Who is by thy beauties undone?" The voice is Joseph's. Without comment or transition, Fielding sets in sequence the singer, the absurd song, Aeschylus, and the violent spontaneity of three marvelously direct and healthy people who love each other dearly. Adams has been poring unconsciously over his Aeschylus during the song,

> when, casting his eyes on Fanny, he cried out, "Bless us, you look extremely pale!" "Pale! Mr. Adams," says she; "O Jesus!" and fell backwards in her chair. Adams jumped up, flung his Aeschylus into the fire, and fell a-roaring to the people of the house for help.

When Fanny is revived by Joseph's kisses Adams dances about the room "in a rapture of joy" and recollects Aeschylus in time to save only his sheepskin covering. Fanny attempts to make her obeisance to Mrs. Slipslop:

> . . . she curtsied, and offered to advance to her; but that high woman would not return her curtsies; but, casting her eyes another way, immediately withdrew into another room, muttering as she went, "she wondered who the creature was."

Mrs. Slipslop's lofty disdain of Fanny gives Fielding a chance for a brilliant brief exposition of the vertical metaphor he ordinarily prefers to present dramatically. The vertical social figure, the "ladder of dependence" that both connects and divides "*high* people and *low* people," naturally involves itself with a metaphor of clothing, and it intersects the horizontal metaphor of traveling and conveyance. High people dress richly and ride high. Low people wear what they can find and walk level with the earth; it behooves them to "find their legs as nimble as they desire." The social world is made up of people of fashion and people of no fashion; and ". . . so far from looking on each other as brethren in the Christian language," high and low "seem scarce to regard each other as of the same species." In a dozen dense lines Fielding sketches his "ladder of dependence," a ladder of costume and attendance, mounting from postillion to sovereign; then he pronounces his own bemused and chagrined judgment: ". . . perhaps, if the gods, according to the opinion of some, made men only to laugh at them, there is no part of our behaviour which answers the end of our creation better than this." Joseph, Fanny, and Adams know very well that their place is near the foot of the ladder. But their real separation from the ranks above is not social but spiritual. They accept their lowness amiably and indulge in no vulgar efforts to climb because they find themselves fully and passionately occupied where loftiness is measured by another standard. Their kind of low loftiness is possible only to the pure in heart.

After a hearty quarrel with the lofty Slipslop, Adams retires to nap out the night in his chair, solaced by three pipes and quantities of ale. Left alone at last the lovers agree to a formal engagement, and Joseph, behaving with that precipitancy he shares with Adams, "leapt up in a rapture, and awakened the parson, earnestly begging that he would that instant join their hands together." But there he has run plump against the point in which the lowly Adams is rigorously high, the ordained ceremonies of the church.

Adams rebuked him for his request, and told him, "He would
by no means consent to anything contrary to the forms of the
Church; that he had no license, nor indeed would he advise him
to obtain one. That the Church had prescribed a form—namely,
the publication of banns—with which all good Christians ought
to comply, and to the omission of which he attributed the many
miseries which befell great folks in marriage. . . ."

The three are prevented from leaving the inn by their customary pennilessness, which Fielding renders in a burlesque
anatomy of their "account":

	£	s.	d.
Mr. Adams and company, Dr. __	o	7	o
In Mr. Adams' pocket _____	o	o	6½
In Mr. Joseph's _____	o	o	o
In Miss Fanny's _____	o	o	o
Balance	o	6	5½

Adams "whipt out on his toes," learns of a wealthy brother
clergyman in the neighborhood, and sets out confidently to
borrow the needed money.

Fielding's ensuing chapter of Parson Adams and Parson
Trulliber is one of the most brilliantly brutal exempla of the
novel. Like all his major episodes it incorporates most of his
central motives. At the outset he plays a curious and bitter
trick with his high-low metaphor: he gives Trulliber most of
his height in girth: the general grasping ingestiveness which
has given him his wealth and height in the world has taken the
visible symbolic form of his great belly. He is a squat swine of
a man, "his shadow ascending very near as far in height, when
he lay on his back, as when he stood on his legs." On market
days it is not easy to tell him from his own fat porkers. In
what I take to be a dreadful parody of the communion celebration, Fielding discovers Trulliber stripped to his waistcoat,
wearing a farm apron, "just come from serving his hogs."
Willingly mistaking Adams for a pig buyer, Trulliber insists

that he handle his wares, and the accommodating Adams is pulled headlong in the mire of the sty. It is perhaps the rudest of the many assaults to which the emblematic cassock is subjected. But the sacred garment is impervious to the world's filth, though the world may choose to deride it, as Trulliber does: " 'Ay, ay . . . I perceive you have some cassock; I will not venture to caale it a whole one.' " Wolfing his food and ale, and denying his charity, Trulliber is full of high sentence about "the cloth," and he shares the world's view of the right way to travel: " '. . . I assure you I don't love to see clergymen on foot; it is not seemly nor suiting the dignity of the cloth.' " When he learns that Adams has really come to borrow fourteen shillings Trulliber would like to strip him of his cassock for running about as a penniless vagabond. Adams retires defeated to the inn, after Mrs. Trulliber has begged her husband "not to fight, but show himself a true Christian, and take the law of him." Back at the inn the travelers are again sent on their way by a poor peddler who lends them his last six shillings and sixpence.

Fielding spends the remaining two chapters of his second volume in what seems a continuing effort to instruct the uninstructable Adams in the uncharitable wickedness of men and the deceptiveness of books as guides to motives. The travelers fall in with a local squire who blandly, and with all appropriate moral sentiments, offers them a series of favors ranging from a night's lodging to a new living for Adams worth three hundred pounds a year. At first it appears that Fielding means to set the extreme of generosity alongside Trulliber's extreme of vulgar greediness. But it quickly develops that every hearty promise was false, and that the squire is notorious for a long history of these deceptions, some of them disastrous to innocent people. Fielding does not explain him, he simply leaves him hanging in our minds as a piece of disturbing pathology or cynicism. The episode demonstrates again, in any case, that true charity is above all else a deed, an affair of works. And it shows Adams' special helplessness, in his bookish ignorance of the real world, to see into a psychology and a morality as devious as this. The pragmatic Joseph's suspicions rise quickly at the squire's rich promises, and the host of the inn, a ruined shipmaster with his own sad knowledge of falsehood, advises that men's faces prove only whether or not they have had the small-pox. But Adams holds blindly to his point, in the vanity of learning which is his special contribution to the novel's satirical motive: " '. . . knowledge of men is only to be learnt from books: Plato and Seneca for that; and those are authors, I am afraid, child, you never read.' "

In his chapter introductory to Book III, "Matter prefatory in praise of biography," Fielding claims for his moral fable the kind of representativeness that is fundamental both to satire and to comedy. He has insisted all along that he is writing biography, an account of lives, and he makes clear now the round emblematic sense in which he means the word.

> I describe not men, but manners; not an individual but a species. Perhaps it will be answered, Are not the characters taken from life? To which I answer in the affirmative; nay, I believe I might aver that I have writ little more than I have seen. The lawyer is not only alive, but hath been so these four thousand years. . . .

Having survived four thousand years, the legendary time of man, the lawyer becomes a Platonic type of something constant in human nature. Precisely so with the "coeval" Mrs. Tow-wouse:

> . . . and, though, perhaps, during the changes which so long an existence must have passed through, she may in turn have stood behind the bar in an inn, I will not scruple to affirm she hath likewise in the revolution of ages sat on a throne. In short, where extreme turbulency of temper, avarice, and an insensibility of human misery, with a degree of hypocrisy, have united in a female composition, Mrs. Tow-wouse was that woman. . . .

Fielding's intention of moral satire is conscious and plain:

". . . we mean not to lash individuals, but all of the like sort. . . ." Thus, treating not men but manners, the book attacks lamentable forms of the race,

> . . . to hold the glass to thousands in their closets, that they may contemplate their deformity, and endeavour to reduce it, and then by suffering private mortification may avoid public shame. This places the boundary between, and distinguishes the satirist from the libeller. . . .

It is perfectly clear how hearteningly far from "lewd and ungenerous" was Fielding's moving spirit, and how far his purpose has advanced beyond the parodying of a possibly irritating but probably harmless novel by Samuel Richardson.

In his resumed narrative Fielding touches lightly and ironically on the ideas of his prefatory chapter. He works negatively, for example, and in harmony with his running jest with the reader, by refusing to specify the route of the travelers. "The reader must excuse me if I am not particular as to the way they took," he says, and goes on to explain that he wants to prevent "malicious persons" from identifying Booby-Hall with any particular seat or any particular family of country squires—a race for whom he protests a general affection. This studious anonymity is the ultimate in treating not men but manners; and by calling attention to his own vagueness of specification Fielding intensifies the hard but general light of satire upon an unnamed but fully recognized and severely typified object. And, as is proper to the gay and serious moral intention, the vague route turns symbolic. That we are traveling from London to Somersetshire is enough to tell us that we are going from town to country, from confusion to simplicity, and that the three simple travelers our companions are seeking their natural and spiritual home. Without pressing the matter, the nameless way becomes a comic Tao, *the* way.

In Fielding, Tao must straggle through the hobbledehoy landscape of country comedy, and in the next episode the travelers proceed through a pitch-dark night, Adams lamenting the loss of his Aeschylus until he is reminded that if he had it he could not read it. Adams tumbles head over heels down a steep hill, landing typically unharmed; Joseph then picks up Fanny in his arms and walks with her firmly and sedately to the bottom of the same hill. The paired images of the descent, Joseph's and Adams', are burlesque versions of Fielding's travel theme, and of high and low people. And he quickly applies the same incident to his theme of bodily and spiritual health, *Mens sana*:

> Learn hence, my fair countrywomen, to consider your own weakness, and the many occasions on which the strength of a man may be useful to you; and, duly weighing this, take care that you match not yourselves with the spindle-shanked beaus and *petit-maîtres* of the age, who, instead of being able, like Joseph Andrews, to carry you in lusty arms through the rugged ways and downhill steeps of life, will rather want to support their feeble limbs with your strength and assistance.

After he has convinced their next host of the genuineness of his cassock by reading a long and circumstantial lecture on the *Iliad* and "rapping out" a hundred Greek verses, Adams persuades him to tell them his "history." It develops that the host's name is Wilson, and he is so called no more casually than the parson is named Abraham Adams.* The history, and the episode in which it is set, are richly exemplary. Left "master" of himself at sixteen when his father died, young Wilson took possession of his fortune, left school, and set out to be a "fine gentleman" alone in London: "And to this early introduction into life, without a guide, I impute all my future misfortunes. . . ." The history is the archetypal rake's progress: vanity, profligacy, wasted health and wasted fortune, ending in imprisonment for debt, significantly at the suit of his tailor. He was saved from prison by his distant cousin, one Harriet Hearty, and after marriage the two tried and failed in the

---

* "Pilgrim, patriarch, and priest," Martin C. Battestin rightly calls him in his introduction to the Riverside Edition. "I am the father of six, and have been of eleven," Adam says.

wine trade, then invested their little remaining fortune in the country place where they had lived for twenty years, retired "from a world full of bustle, noise, hatred, envy, and ingratitude, to ease, quiet, and love." Their peaceful country tenure, Wilson avers, has been idyllic except for the kidnapping by gypsies of their eldest son, a lad whom he would know among ten thousand, "for he had a mark in his left breast of a strawberry, which his mother had given him by longing for that fruit." After a morning spent in inspecting the Wilsons' self-sufficient rural husbandry Adams believes that already he has rediscovered the life of the Golden Age. But Fielding has already carefully marred the idyll by the brutal incident of the shooting of little Miss Wilson's spaniel by the young squire of the neighboring manor. The country retreat is no more immune than the city to cruelty and ill-nature.

The travelers take up their way, with much fine talk in which Joseph figures more boldly than formerly, of education and of charity. Adams defends private tuition, in which he considers himself one of the great masters, against the vanities and immorality of the public schools, then goes sound asleep during Joseph's peroration on charity and its infrequent occurrence, and awakens to find himself and his cassock being pulled about by a pack of hounds who have pursued a hare into his neighborhood. Fielding applies his most gorgeous mock-heroic diction to describe the havoc wrought by Joseph and his cudgel in rescuing the parson. The cudgel, for example, becomes a kind of anti-Shield of Achilles, as Fielding limns in detail the scenes which were designed to be carved there but which were omitted for lack of room. The three travelers are taken home for dinner by the hunting squire and his pack of human curs, who see in Adams a promising butt and in Fanny a handsome and helpless female. From the "scene of roasting very nicely adapted to the present taste and times" which ensues—a series of vulgar practical jokes conceived by the latest of Fielding's loathsome squires, a product of home tutelage and French foppery—Adams emerges with his cassock further battered but his dignity and resolution unimpaired. When the squire sends his cur-companions after the travelers to the inn where they are sheltering, another epical battle ensues in which, among other violent strokes, Joseph breaks an immense chamber-pot over the head of the captain, so that "he fell prostrate on the floor with a lumpish noise, and his halfpence rattled in his pocket"—Fielding's delicious diminutive of the refrain of the *Iliad*, "and his armor clanged upon him." Joseph and Adams are finally borne down by superior numbers and Fanny is carried off by the squire's creatures, leaving her friends tied back to back to the bedposts, a posture in which Adams has leisure to drive Joseph nearly mad with circumstantial descriptions of Fanny's likely fate and counsels of Christian patience.

Fanny is rescued in good time by outriders of Peter Pounce, Lady Booby's usurious bailiff, and is taken into the chariot of that great man, who of course rides high. Now, with the journey nearing its destination, Fielding brings his major metaphors strongly to bear. The sartorial state of Adams, as he confronts the magnificent Peter, stands at its most lamentable: he wears neither breeches nor stockings, his battered wig is bound about with a red spotted handkerchief, his torn cassock dangles below his greatcoat, and his face shows familiarity with the contents of a chamber-pot and a scrub-bucket. Peter Pounce "advised him to make himself clean, nor would accept his homage in that pickle." Adams has lost everything but the dignity of his "cloth," which he knows is a matter of content not of form. Now modes of conveyance are heavily discussed and in the upshot much manipulated. Peter Pounce wants Fanny in his chariot; Fanny wishes to ride behind Joseph on Adams' horse, now restored to him at last, and Adams urges this too; Joseph refuses to ride unless Adams is provided for; Peter, abandoning hope of Fanny, finally takes Adams into his chariot, and "the whole procession set forwards for Booby-

Hall." But Fielding devises a quarrel to prevent his travelers' arriving in this unfamiliar elegance. Peter and Adams discuss charity, which Adams now formally defines as " 'a generous disposition to relieve the distressed.' " Peter rather approves his phrasing: " '. . . it is, as you say, a disposition—and does not so much consist in the act as in the disposition to do it. . . .' " Peter's violent response to Adams' unpardonable doubt of his great wealth allows Fielding to restore the parson, who "in his heart . . . preferred the *pedestrian* even to the *vehicular* expedition," to the services of his own feet:

> "Sir," said *Adams*, "I value not your chariot of a rush; and if I had known you intended to affront me, I would have walked to the world's end on foot ere I would have accepted a place in it. However, sir, I will soon rid you of that inconvenience"; and, so saying, he opened the chariot door, without calling to the coachman, and lept out into the highway, forgetting to take his hat along with him; which, however, Mr. Pounce threw after him with great violence.

Joseph and Fanny "stopt to bear him company," and the final mile to the country parish, the scene of the concluding action, is appropriately traversed on foot.

Close on their heels arrives Lady Booby in her coach and six. Fielding sharply distinguishes her reception from that accorded Parson Adams:

> She entered the parish amidst the ringing of bells, and the acclamations of the poor, who were rejoiced to see their patroness returned after so long an absence, during which time all her rents had been drafted to London, without a shilling being spent among them, which tended not a little to their utter impoverishing. . . .

This is the "public joy" motivated by "interest"—need, gain. Toward Adams the people are moved by shy and pure "affection," they surround him physically, desiring a touch or a word:

> They flocked about him like dutiful children round an indul-

gent parent, and vied with each other in demonstrations of duty
and love. The parson on his side shook everyone by the hand,
inquiring heartily after the healths of all that were absent, of
their children and relations; and exprest a satisfaction in his
face which nothing but benevolence made happy by its objects
could infuse.

It is plain in what grand and homely sense we are to understand Abraham Adams as patriarch and priest.

As pilgrim he has ostensibly, but only ostensibly, completed
his task. The physical journey is ended but the spiritual one is
not yet fulfilled. The cursive themes and figures of the pilgrimage are all collected now in one place; and whereas the
basic movement of the action is still horizontal, it now turns
lateral, from side to side rather than forward. In the sense
that the visible conflict now again lies between the corrupt
passion of Lady Booby for Joseph and the pure passion of
Joseph and Fanny, the action of the novel has returned to
its beginning. Tension still comes from the intersecting and
interrupting vertical drives: the interests of the high folk of
that high place Booby-Hall intersect the interests of the low
folk of Adams' spreading country parish. But the low folk of
the parish have their high place, too—the church; and there
Parson Adams takes on a formidable height of his own. In his
church, in his surplice, Adams abruptly sheds all absurdity.

Priest and patroness soon confront head-on when Adams
first publishes the marriage banns of "Joseph Andrews and
Frances Goodwill, both of this parish," and Lady Booby pe-
remptorily forbids him, on pain of dismissal, to proceed in the
marriage. " 'I tell you a reason,' " says she: " 'he is a vagabond, and he shall not settle here, and bring a nest of beggars
into the parish; it will make us but little amends that they will
be beauties.' " To Fielding's design it matters greatly that
Joseph and Fanny shall marry, and that they shall produce
children who shall be beauties. It is the kind of stock his world
needs, as the whole action of his story has insisted. Adams'
response is prompt and proud:

"Madam, . . . I know not what your ladyship means by the terms 'master' and 'service.' I am in the service of a Master who will never discard me for doing my duty; and if the doctor (for indeed I have never been able to pay for a licence) thinks proper to turn me out from my cure, God will provide me, I hope, another. At least, my family, as well as myself, have hands; and he will prosper, I doubt not, our endeavours to get our bread honestly with them. Whilst my conscience is pure, I shall never fear what man can do to me."

And though it is "with many bows, or at least many attempts at a bow" that he takes his leave, we are aware of a new grandeur in him specific to function. The making of an elegant leg is no part of his duty to his Master. Next church day "Mr. *Adams* published the banns again with as audible a voice as before."

By coach and six, perforce, Fielding at last brings on the scene his version, by now only temperately sardonic, of Richardson's Pamela and her Mr. B., nephew to our Lady Booby. Mr. Booby shortly begins to raise Joseph toward his sister Pamela's new eminence by habiting him in "a suit of his own clothes, with linen and other necessaries. . . ." Joseph chooses the plainest available costume, "a blue coat and breeches, with a gold edging, and a red waistcoat with the same"; since the suit is large for Mr. Booby, Joseph fills it out handsomely, and appears for the first time in clothing suited to his "natural gentility." Fielding pretends to be so dazzled by his hero's new finery that he resolves henceforward to call him Mr. Joseph, "he having as good a title to that appellation as many others— I mean that incontested one of good clothes"; but he quickly and pointedly allows that genteel intention to go by default. When Adams sees Joseph so dressed out he "burst into tears with joy, and fell to rubbing his hands and snapping his fingers, as if he had been mad." Mr. Booby presents Joseph to his aunt, " 'dressed like a gentleman, in which light I intend he shall hereafter be seen.' " But Fielding will not have gentlemen made this way, by tailors. Joseph's new habit was "indeed not wanted to set off the lively colours in which Nature had drawn health, strength, comeliness, and youth." To these physical qualities of the essential Joseph, the gifts of God, he has himself joined the gentleman's modesty, candor, and manly courage. He is not tempted to alter his nature to accord with his clothes. " 'I am resolved on no account to quit my dear Fanny,' " he rebuffs the squire; " 'no, though I could raise her as high above her present station as you have raised my sister.' " In contrast to Pamela, who has embraced with rapture the opportunity to rise in the world, Joseph's highest wish is to support Fanny with his labor in " 'that station to which she was born, and with which she is content.' "

After he has quitted the company of Booby-Hall in disgust, and after he has rescued Fanny from the violently lecherous little gentleman Beau Didapper, the bloody Joseph takes refuge with the flustered Fanny at the home of Adams, who, after he has "presented" Fanny "a bone of bacon he had just been gnawing, being the only remains of his provision," lectures them again on their incontinent desire to hasten their marriage, the sin of carnal appetite, and the duty of submission to the will of Providence: "for he was a great enemy to the passions, and preached nothing more than the conquest of them by reason and grace." Adams instances the submission of the earlier Abraham in the sacrifice of Isaac; then this marvelously passionate enemy of the passions, hearing that his little son is drowned, storms about in an ecstasy of grief, and when the boy is rescued he rejoices with the same "extravagance": ". . . he kissed and embraced his son a thousand times, and danced about the room like one frantic. . . ." When he has recovered his poise Adams resumes his counsels of "moderation and discretion" in love; but Joseph is afraid he will never succeed in loving Fanny moderately. Mrs. Adams, speaking for Fielding and all true hearts, closes the scene: " 'Don't hearken to him, Mr. Joseph; be as good a husband as you are able, and love your wife with all your body and soul too.' "

75

After the departure of Lady Booby's slumming party, who have come to laugh at "one of the most ridiculous sights they had ever seen, which was an old foolish parson, who . . . kept a wife and six brats on a salary of about twenty pounds a year," good nature enjoys one of its own pure intervals when Joseph escorts the whole parsonage party across to the George, "where he had bespoke a piece of bacon and greens for their dinner."

After a final grand efflorescence of bedroom slapstick, there ensues the revelation that Fanny is in fact the lost sister of Pamela and thus on the point of making an incestuous union with her own brother; then the revelation that Joseph is in fact not an Andrews at all but the lost son of Mr. Wilson, identified by the presence on his bosom which, "when a boy, was as white as driven snow; and, where it is not covered with hairs, is so still," of that strawberry mark "which his mother had given him by longing for that fruit." The event parodies, I suppose, not only the creaky conventions of romantic plotting, but the Aristotelian "discovery"; and it parodies, in comedy made rich by accumulated meaning and feeling, the reunion of the Biblical Joseph and his father. As Mr. Wilson embraces Joseph with the cry, " 'I have discovered my son, I have him again in my arms!' " and Joseph throws himself at his father's feet and begs his blessing, Adams capers about the room shouting, " 'Hic est quem quæris; inventus est, etc.' " We are meant to feel the divine workings, and we do so, not in spite of but through the comedy.

Fielding's summary chapter of the wedding and its aftermath, with which we began, is not a casual bundling of the lines of action, with descriptive decoration. It is the dramatized proof of an extended moral proposition, a completed Beatitude, furnished with the novel's now habitual data, at once quotidian and exemplary, metaphors richly common. When the love of Joseph and Fanny culminates in marriage, by Parson Adams, followed by a day of celebration of utmost merriment corrected by the strictest decency, Fielding is consummating what he has had dramatically to say of the seemly behavior of men of good will. Joseph must lead Fanny, on foot, to and from the altar, and he must go in "a neat, but plain suit" and she in "nothing richer than a white dimity nightgown." The full-blooded good health of the whole affair will be expressed in her "little straw hat, lined with cherry-coloured silk, and tied with a cherry-coloured ribbon." That is the brightest as well as the purest color we have seen, as it should be. If vulgar high persons laugh during the ceremony, they must expect to be publicly rebuked, for "Mr. Adams at church with his surplice on, and Mr. Adams without that ornament, in any other place, were two very different persons." With his surplice laid away, Mr. Adams is shortly "well filled with ale and pudding." And Joseph, having made his crucial pilgrimage, knows when he has reached the end of it, and knows he is right to stay there, with Fanny managing his dairy, though she will soon be a bit hampered by being very big with her first child.

Smollett's Healing Journey

N THE attractively repulsive opening sentence of *The Expedition of Humphry Clinker* the speaker is Smollett's valetudinarian hero, Old Squaretoes Matthew Bramble, who thinks of himself as "prematurely superannuated" at fifty-five, after having studied his own case "with the most painful attention" during the fourteen years in which he has carried "an hospital" within himself. He writes from Gloucester to Dr. Dick Lewis, his old friend and physician back home in Wales:

> The pills are good for nothing—I might as well swallow snowballs to cool my reins—I have told you over and over how hard I am to move; and at this time of day, I ought to know something of my own constitution.

In his last letter, approaching Gloucester again from the North, three seasons and some hundreds of miles later, he writes:

> As I have laid in a considerable stock of health, it is to be hoped you will not have much trouble with me in the way of physic, but I intend to work you on the side of exercise.—I have got an excellent fowling-piece from Mr. Lismahago, who is a keen sportsman, and we shall take the heath in all weathers.

The movement of the Expedition in space has been roughly circular: the traveling party has returned, much changed, to its point of departure. But the spiritual movement has been resolutely straight ahead, on and out. The reward of experi-

78

ence, according to *Four Quartets*, is to return to a place and know it for the first time. What has altered is not the place but the vision, not the known but the knower: one knows the place now because one knows the self better. The design of *Humphry Clinker* has been described by Robert Gorham Davis as "a movement of reconciliation," and it is that among other things. The action of the novel is best understood under a figure of winnowing—an airing and sifting and sorting and settling, which alters the state and relation of things. The action moves from negative to positive, from passive to active: sickness to health, constipation to purgation, irritability to sensitivity, anonymity to identity, distance to intimacy, doubt to trust, celibacy to marriage, ignorance to knowledge.

In what remains of his first letter Matthew Bramble reveals most of his other tensions as well as some of the virtues and powers which may save him. He is "equally distressed," he says, "in mind and body." He has yet to learn how closely the two are related, as halves of the whole he must create. A fretful and sickly bachelor, he has been saddled with an orphan niece and nephew, products of the lamentable fertility of others: "As if I had not plagues enough of my own, those children of my sister are left me for a perpetual source of vexation—what business have people to get children to plague their neighbors?" Apparently what he hates and fears is life itself, and his sister's children as animated emblems of life. He frets in that slow suicidal state in which every motion is anticipated as part of a pattern understood as fated and malign. "I shall set out to-morrow morning for the Hot Well at Bristol, where I am afraid I shall stay longer than I could wish." So far, so hopeless. But what will save him is love, a loving heart. Perhaps it is himself he hates, not life, not persons. Now he gives orders for a series of charitable gestures, as helplessly demanded by his loving inner nature as is his irritability by his unease: "Tell Barns to thresh out the two old ricks, and send the corn to market, and sell it off to the poor at a shilling a bushel under market price"; "Let Morgan's widow have the Alderney cow, and forty shillings to clothe her children: but don't say a syllable of the matter to any living soul"; his suit against his purse-proud neighbor Griffin is to be withdrawn in exchange for five pounds given to the poor of the parish.

Matthew Bramble is not alone in his neediness, and the motives of the Expedition are not fully visible until the other travelers have spoken in their early letters. Sister Tabitha, Mr. Bramble's "perpetual grind-stone," writes to her housekeeper at Brambleton-hall in terms of her own major vices, vanity and cupidity, demanding her most killing clothes and giving orders for various parsimonious measures. She requires also a "lacksitif" for her loathsome dog Chowder, "terribly constuprated ever since we left huom." What ails Chowder, who embodies a low-comedy animal equivalent of Matthew Bramble's high-comedy human malaise, is in fact the family malady. When Win Jenkins, Tabby's maid, writes much later, "O Mary! the whole family have been in such a constipation!" she means "consternation," but the phrase carries the force of a Freudian slip. Likewise the higher illiteracy of Tabitha's first letter: ". . . don't forget to have the gate shit every evening before dark"; and, "I know that hussy, Mary Jones, loves to be rumping with the men." Here as elsewhere, Smollett is indulging heartily in the enthusiastic intestinal humor of his era; but his purpose is serious as well as comic. He means us to understand his creatures' need of purgation in various forms.

On a first view Matthew Bramble has seen his nephew " 'squire Jery" as "a pert jackanapes, full of college-petulance and self-conceit; proud as a German count, and as hot and hasty as a Welch mountaineer." Both the subject and the reader are in need of correction. Young Jery Melford's own first letter, like his uncle's and his sister's, suggests the good and the bad material upon which the action must work. He is a bit complacent, a bit arrogant, a bit precipitate, but promisingly open and available in the region of the heart and mind. He is quite able to see at once that he has got into "a family of originals," and to accept the accident positively, as conducive not merely to exasperation but to amusement and instruction. His first judgment of Matthew Bramble is peevish and shallow: "My uncle is an odd kind of humourist, always on the fret, and so unpleasant in his manner, that rather than be obliged to keep him company, I'd resign all claim to the inheritance of his estate." But he quickly reminds himself that the squire's prickliness may bear a relation to his gout, and that there may be reasons not yet clear to him why his uncle is revered by his servants and his neighbors "even to a degree of enthusiasm."

In her softer way his sister Liddy is undergoing the same correction of view. "My uncle, who was so dreadfully passionate in the beginning, has been moved by my tears and distress," she writes to her school mistress; "and is now all tenderness and compassion." "Having no mother of my own," she begins that pitiful little letter begging forgiveness for her secret but innocuous intrigue with the "stroller" Wilson. Her sins are few and small. ". . . I found her a fine, tall girl, of seventeen, with an agreeable person," Jery reports; "but remarkably simple, and quite ignorant of the world." In her uncle's view, ". . . she's deficient in spirit, and so susceptible— and so tender forsooth!—truly, she has got a languishing eye, and reads romances." She needs only to grow up a bit, in a word; and she would be the better for a parent. So would her brother Jery, with his faults of the opposite order.

Thinking of the two of them and of Tabby, Matthew Bramble wonders what he has done to deserve "such family-plagues." ". . . why the devil should not I shake off these torments at once?" he complains. "I an't married to Tabby, thank Heaven! nor did I beget the other two: let them choose another guardian. . . ." But before the letter is over, as he describes Liddy's dangerous illness following the uproar about her little affair, he again helplessly reveals the inner man:

"You cannot imagine what I have suffered, partly from the indiscretion of this poor child, but much more from the fear of losing her entirely."

Smollett's comic action, then, shows a group of persons, separately and collectively disordered, forcibly joined, seeking a serenity and wholeness which will both allow them to compose a family and to stand free as individuals.

Within two weeks Jery and his uncle have begun to move toward an understanding. "The truth is," as the young man puts it, "his disposition and mine, which, like oil and vinegar, repelled one another at first, have now begun to mix by dint of being beat up together." The rapprochement is not merely forcible and imposed. Jery's natural penetration and sympathy have begun to seek nourishment. He sees that his uncle's sickness is real and that its roots are complex. "I think his peevishness arises partly from bodily pain, and partly from a natural excess of morbid sensibility. . . ." Excessive, in the sense of extraordinary, it alway is, and at this stage frequently morbid. But Jery shortly sees the unmorbid work of Matthew Bramble's excess of feeling when he spies upon his uncle attempting in private to relieve the need of a widow with a consumptive child. The termagant Tabby, interrupting the scene, will not believe that something so benign as charity is going forward. "Who gives twenty pounds in charity?" she rages. "But you are a stripling—You know nothing of the world." About Jery's ignorance she is right in the main; but he has found in Tabitha Bramble a monitory example, and in Matthew Bramble a noble exemplar to whom he responds with his own promising excess. Watching the scene he is moved to tears, and he wishes to add his bit to his uncle's benevolence.

Jery's maturity advances step by step with his appreciation of his uncle's character, which "opens and improves upon me every day." Matthew Bramble's character itself is "improving" with improved health, as his imposing richness finds freedom to express itself in speech and action; and Jery's improving ability to feel and to value the prickly beauty of his uncle's nature measures the enriching of his own spirit. Both processes are parts of the spiritual progress of the Expedition, rhythmically advancing and thickening with its movement. In three weeks' exposure Jery has learned a great deal:

> His singularities afford a rich mine of entertainment; his understanding, so far as I can judge, is well cultivated: his observations on life are equally just, pertinent, and uncommon. He affects misanthropy, in order to conceal the sensibility of a heart, which is tender, even to a degree of weakness.

Jery has already made the discriminations necessary to carry him strongly forward. Shortly he finds both deeper insights and the precision of phrase that comes from just and accurate sympathy: "He is as tender as a man without a skin," he writes of his uncle on April 30. He qualifies crucially his judgment of Mr. Bramble's misanthropy: "He is the most risible misanthrope I ever met with." Risibility, again, is a power fundamental to them both, one of the inner essences that fit them to make their Expedition with profit. The lad is beginning to understand, as well, Matthew Bramble's purgative need, his desperate requirement of an object outside himself; and the intimate reciprocity of his psyche and his soma: ". . . when his spirits are not exerted externally, they seem to recoil and prey upon himself."

The younger and eminently girlish Liddy, meanwhile, rescued from her decline by her uncle's solicitude and heartened by a loving message from the mysterious Wilson, falls frequently into an exquisitely trite vein of finishing-school prose, exactly like the waters she drinks from "the *nymph of Bristol spring*," "so clear, so pure, so mild, so charmingly maukish," an idiom appropriate to the surface of her undeveloped nature:

> . . . the Downs are so agreeable; the furze in full blossom; the ground enamelled with daisies, and primroses, and cowslips; all the trees bursting into leaves, and the hedges already clothed

with their vernal livery; the mountains covered with flocks of sheep and tender bleating wanton lambkins playing, frisking, and skipping from side to side; the groves resound with the notes of blackbird, thrush, and linnet; and all night long sweet Philomel pours forth her ravishingly delightful song.

At this stage she can describe love and friendship, without embarrassment, as "charming passions," and give as presents a heart-housewife and a tortoise-shell memorandum book. She is leading a life of factitious romantic sensation, from the outside in. "The eye is continually entertained with the splendour of dress and equipage; and the ear with the sound of coaches, chaises, chairs, and other carriages," she writes on a first view of Bath. But fortunately Liddy too is showing the indispensable organ, a loving heart, and her right reading of her uncle's nature bespeaks her own inner soundness.

Matthew Bramble's illness, of body and spirit, is real, and there is nothing facile or perfunctory about his recovery. Jery's word, misanthropy, is one Mr. Bramble often applies to himself in the early stages of the travels. "Heark ye, Lewis, my misanthropy increases every day," he writes from Bath on April 28. And he roundly asks, "But what have I to do with the human species?" To the mob and the filth at Bath he reacts in a rhapsody of rage and disgust. But he already realizes that he must attribute much of the blackness of his view to an "exaggerated impression on the irritable nerves of an invalid." He is humorously shamed by the querulous tone of his letters, and suggests calling them *the lamentations of Matthew Bramble.* Still he understands the letters as therapy and feels the purgative value of free complaint: ". . . it is no small alleviation of my grievances, that I have a sensible friend, to whom I can communicate my crusty humours, which, by retention, would grow intolerably acrimonious."

Mr. Bramble's "nerves of uncommon sensibility" are not yet fortified to withstand a general assault. As he overlooks a ball at Bath, "the multitude rising at once" to prepare for the country-dances, "the whole atmosphere was put in commotion," and Mr. Bramble faints dead away. But the test was severe:

> Imagine to yourself a high exalted essence of mingled odours, arising from putrid gums, imposthumated lungs, sour flatulencies, rank arm-pits, sweating feet, running sores and issues, plasters, ointments, and embrocations, hungary-water, spirit of lavender, assafoetida drops, musk, hartshorn, and sal volatile; besides a thousand frowzy steams, which I could not analyse.

The essential healthy turning outward of his nature, which began with his forbearing interest in his young wards and has continued in his affection for several old cronies found resurrected at Bath, takes grand form in his resolution to extend the Expedition at large. "In an evil hour," as he puts it, he has agreed to carry the party to London, but it is with a good grace that he proposes, with a view to his wards' education, "to make a circuit of all the remarkable scenes" of "this unwieldy metropolis"; and it is upon his own initiative that he decides to travel on into the North: ". . . I think, it is a reproach upon me, as a British freeholder, to have lived so long without making an excursion to the other side of the Tweed." When Chowder is "lost for want of exercise" and Tabitha resolves to supply his need with a daily airing upon the Downs in a post-chaise, the event is seen as farcical; but the spirit, if not the body, can be usefully aired in a post-chaise, and the ventilation of Mr. Bramble's needy little party is now well begun.

The journey to London is notable chiefly for the accession of Humphry Clinker, who joins the travelers as temporary postilion and quickly offends the ladies by showing his bare arse through a rent in his rags. Thereby he makes the discovery, attested by Win Jenkins, of "a skin as fair as alabaster," that ensign so fundamental to the lost child in eighteenth century writings. Smollett brings Humphry swiftly into the pattern of his themes of health, family, charity. Humphry explains himself as a bastard and an orphan, "a love-begotten babe," rendered destitute by illness from which he is not yet perfectly recovered:

> '. . . I am a poor Wiltshire lad—I ha'n't a shirt in the world, that I can call my own, nor a rag of clothes, and please your ladyship, but what you see—I have no friend nor relation upon earth to help me out—I have had the fever and the ague these six months, and spent all I had in the world upon doctors, and to keep soul and body together; and, saving your ladyship's good presence, I han't broke bread these four and twenty hours.'

Thus he is an object precisely calculated to call out the best in Matthew Bramble. " 'Heark ye, Clinker, you are a most notorious offender—You stand convicted of sickness, hunger, wretchedness, and want,' " he salutes him; and when Humphry has run over the long catalogue of his country skills: " 'Foregad! thou art a complete fellow. . . . I have a good mind to take thee into my family.' " Mr. Bramble means his family of servants. Tabitha spitefully continues the metaphor: " ' . . . the world shall see whether you have more regard for your own flesh and blood, or for a beggarly foundling taken from the dunghill.' " Smollett has prepared the irony which both must discover, that Clinker is both a beggarly foundling and Matthew Bramble's flesh and blood.

London is not new to Mr. Bramble, an old Parliament man, but he is startled and offended by its sprawling growth during the term of his willing rustication in Wales. "What I left open fields, producing hay and corn, I now find covered with streets and squares, and palaces, and churches." Not surprisingly, he sees the city in terms of sickness and monstrosity: ". . . the capital is become an overgrown monster; which, like a dropsical head, will in time leave the body and extremities without nourishment and support"; and again: ". . . this chaos, this misshapen and monstrous capital, without head or tail, members or proportion." He is disgusted by the grossness and disorder, the pushing display of low ambition and systematic deceit. Everywhere is the busy self-serving mob, "this incongruous monster called *the public*," "rambling, riding, rolling, rushing, justling, mixing, bouncing, cracking, and crashing in one vile ferment of stupidity and corruption." Like his great contemporary Samuel Johnson, he deplores a formless social structure without "distinction or subordination," in which no man knows his duty but every man knows his interest. He fears the leveling influence of the mob, as Jery sees, because he finds it "incompatible with excellence, and subversive of order."

Equally predictably, Liddy is "quite in a maze of admiration" after a short exposure to "the wonders of this vast metropolis" where "the imagination is quite confounded with splendour and variety." Ranelagh delights her as "the inchanted palace of a genie," and at Vauxhall she is "dazzled and confounded with the variety of beauties." She is surprised to find that her uncle "did not seem to relish the place"; but then she bethinks herself, very sensibly: "People of experience and infirmity, my dear Letty, see with very different eyes from those that such as you and I make use of."

Yet Mr. Bramble can quite reasonably say, "I flatter myself, the exercise of travelling has been of service to my health. . . ." For whereas his disapproval of London, like his disapproval of Bath, is vehement and detailed, the circumstantiality of Smollett's treatment of the London scene makes a base for a profounder and more considered judgment, a disgust more reasoned and particular. "I am, at present, by a violent effort of the mind, forced from my natural bias," Mr. Bramble writes of his stay in the capital on June 2; "but this power ceasing to act, I shall return to my solitude with redoubled velocity. Every thing I see, and hear, and feel, in this great reservoir of folly, knavery, and sophistication, contributes to inhance the value of a country life. . . ." Bias is not quite the same thing as prejudice, and Matthew Bramble is by now much less prone to prejudge, to flash out in attack along

predictable lines. When in his letter of June 8 he devotes a
half-dozen pages to comparing the solid satisfactions of life at
Brambleton-hall with life in the city "where every corner
teems with fresh objects of detestation and disgust," his account is wholly persuasive. He is confirming an old bias, but
he earns it before our eyes by testing town against country by
rational standards and visible evidence. By seeing his country
life with whole clarity for the first time he acquires the right,
as well as the means, to value it. His disgust with London is
equally earned and pragmatic. The disgusting objects are
there, and Matthew Bramble has been to see them before pro-
nouncing upon them: "We have been at court, and 'change,
and every where; and every where we find food for spleen,
and subject for ridicule."

Mr. Bramble's spleen is doubtless Smollett's spleen, that
tendency so obvious in this writer that Sterne dubbed him
Smelfungus and advised him to see a doctor. Sterne's own book
was "wrote, an' please your worships, against the spleen." But
the action of *Humphry Clinker* suggests that Smollett was
aware of his own spleen, and not fatally fond of it. A doctor
himself, he knew the physician's occasional need to heal himself. *Humphry Clinker* is a healing book, about healing. Like
his Matthew Bramble a risible misanthrope, like Sterne he
prescribed the comic view. He knew the therapeutic value of
laughter, which Sterne described anatomically:

> . . . in order, by a more frequent and more convulsive elevation
> and depression of the diaphragm, and the succussations of the
> intercostal and abdominal muscles in laughter, to drive the *gall*
> and other *bitter juices* from the gall bladder, liver and sweet-
> bread of his majesty's subjects, with all the inimicitious pas-
> sions which belong to them, down into their duodenums.

But Smollett's laughter is not so gentle or so continuous as
Sterne's, not so civilized; it tends to come in raucous and
sardonic bursts. Sterne forgave the mob gladly because it so
kindly and persistently entertained him, but Smollett could not

quite rise to that flexibility. Smollett's view is satirical and closer to Swift's. Swift saw the mob as a failed ideal, an offense of the race against itself; when he looked at it his gorge rose and his heart broke. Smollett, a lesser man and a lesser artist, tended to take the mob, the vulgarity of life, "personally," as an offense against himself. His gorge rose but his heart did not break, and he preferred to find recourse in anger, vituperation, and self-congratulation—smaller passions.

That syndrome is Matthew Bramble's own ailment, and one to which he succumbs in early stages of the Expedition. But all this has finally come to be matter of knowledge for Smollett in this his last book, a set of tendencies he is laboring, in the action of his story, to exorcise and expiate. He makes Matthew Bramble's progress that of a man trying to prove himself a curable misanthrope. It is not the incremental exercise of an inbreeding spleen. Ultimate forgiveness of the mob, implicit in Swift, is impossible for Matthew Bramble because Smollett cannot quite imagine it. What he does achieve is tremendous in its way, a kind of invulnerability, serenity of mind and sweetness of temper, which will let him lead a full and useful life within limits set by biases over which he really has no control. If full acceptance is hopeless, then that aboveness, a wholeness within limits, is a considerable achievement for a man without a skin.

In London Matthew Bramble is cooperating, as amiably as he can, with a phase of the education of that "family" he is beginning to accept with less and less reluctance. Jery views wisely and well, usually in company with his uncle, the whole range of public and polite life in the capital, and he reacts with maturing wit and discrimination. London brings a gradual calming of Liddy's fluttered nerves and a testing of her affection for Wilson by exposure to the suit of the agreeable Barton. Tabitha, at forty-five "declining into the desperate state of celibacy," continues to organize her life about the pursuit of a male, any male, and she has assumed that Barton's suit was addressed to her, not to her niece. Disappointment teaches her only that she must try again. But she has shown a notable improvement in temper after some peremptory instruction from her brother, and has tamely agreed to renounce Chowder to Lady Griskin, who, appropriately, "proposes to bring the breed of him into fashion." London and Chowder deserve each other. Mr. Bramble looks on at first with disgust then with slow tolerance as Humphry Clinker finds the new light of Methodism in Mr. W——'s sermons and commences preacher himself. Humphry's doctrine has a strong effect upon the females of the family, and persuades Win Jenkins, intermittently, that "the pleasures of London are no better than sower whey and stale cyder, when compared to the joys of the new Gerusalem." After Humphry has been freed from his unjust imprisonment in Clerkenwell, where he was dangerously near to converting the whole population, and returns to embrace Matthew Bramble's knees like the prodigal son, causing his patron to take snuff "in some confusion," the party sets out for the North with general willingness.

Mr. Bramble is at last able to face and to phrase the complexity of his sickness. He writes to Dr. Lewis,

> I find my spirits and my health affect each other reciprocally—that is to say, every thing that discomposes my mind, produces a correspondent disorder in my body; and my bodily complaints are remarkably mitigated by those considerations that dissipate the clouds of mental chagrin.

At Harrigate, on the way north, he makes perfunctory trial of the water and again finds it such that "I can hardly mention it without puking." His cure will not come by chemical means. The real nostrum, the comprehensive ventilation of spirit that Smollett subsumes under the figure of "travelling," is being offered to him all the time. The plight of the contrite highwayman Martin presents one such test and opportunity. Jery's description of the scene shows the emblematic way in which uncle and nephew manifest their increasing mutuality of feeling:

> From a certain sparkling in his eyes, I discovered there was more in his heart, than he cared to express with his tongue, in favour of poor Martin; and this was precisely my own feeling, which he did not fail to discern, by the same means of communication.

At Durham their accumulating experience takes the ramshackle form of the veteran Scots lieutenant, Obadiah Lismahago, just back from the Indian wars in America. Like Humphry Clinker, Lismahago is drawn from his first introduction into the novel's configuration of human loneliness, sickness, and need. He appears an incarnate decrepitude, but he manages stoutly his body wrecked by systematic torture. His head looks so peculiar, he explains, because he has been scalped and his skull broken by a tomahawk.

> A joint of one finger had been cut, or rather sawed off with a rusty knife; one of his great toes was crushed into a mash betwixt two stones; some of his teeth were drawn, or dug out with a crooked nail; splintered reeds had been thrust up his nostrils and other tender parts; and the calves of his legs had been blown up with mines of gunpowder dug in his flesh with the sharp point of the tomahawk.

He is careful to make clear that he has not, like his old companion Murphy, been emasculated, and that is enough for Tabby. "An ogling correspondence forthwith commenced between this amiable pair of originals." He is as unbowed as he is bloody, and will accept no sympathy because he sees no occasion for it.

> 'Sir, . . . I am a gentleman; and entered the service as other gentlemen do, with such hopes and ambitions as honourable ambition inspires—If I have not been lucky in the lottery of life, so neither do I think myself unfortunate—I owe to no man a farthing; I can always command a clean shirt, a mutton-chop, and a truss of straw; and when I die, I shall leave effects sufficient to defray the expence of my burial.'

To Matthew Bramble he forms an astonishing and instructive example of fortitude in adversity, of disenchantment without bitterness. Both uncle and nephew at first tolerate this difficult nature, then find themselves drawn to it. Jery says, ". . . Lismahago is a curiosity which I have not yet sufficiently perused. . . ."; and Mr. Bramble, "I have often met with a crab-apple in a hedge, which I have been tempted to eat for its flavour, even while I was disgusted by its austerity." As Tabby pursues her ogling correspondence her brother pursues a disputatious one, in which he finds himself often "confounded, if not convinced," and always profitably stretched and aired.

The rattling pace of the narrative slows in the peregrination of Scotland. Smollett has become the advocate and turns his Expedition frankly and on the whole gracefully to persuasion. As a loving Scot and a loyal Briton, he works to remove the general prejudice against the Scots which he blames upon English ignorance of the land and its people. He speaks first through Jery: "What, between want of curiosity, and traditional sarcasms, the effect of ancient animosity, the people at the other end of the island know as little of Scotland as of Japan." The benighted Tabitha, for example, believes that Scotland can be reached from England only by sea. Smollett scarcely bothers to mask his didacticism, ordering his travelogue now in a series of vignettes full of handy intervals for persuasion. But he works artfully, in an argument textured like the benign national porridge, "a cooling sub-acid, balsamic and mucilaginous." The travelers are helplessly charmed. In three weeks in Scotland Matthew Bramble finds "more kindness, hospitality, and rational entertainment" than he has met anywhere else in the whole of his life, and he determines that if ever he must give up his country retirement he will go to Edinburgh, that "hot-bed of genius" and good fellowship. Jery is impressed both intellectually and romantically, meeting at the hunters' ball in Edinburgh more "handsome females" than he has ever seen in one assembly. Liddy's beauty makes its mark, and as "the Fair Cambrian" she becomes a local toast, "the occasion of much wine-shed."

The Scottish propaganda is not crude, or dull, or blindly partisan, or alien to the central work of the novel; one resents it only mildly as a slight trepidation in the rhythm of the whole and a discord in the established tone. Smollett's concern for the right understanding and the right use of the "union" of Scotland and England was timely when he wrote, and legitimate matter for an Expedition which was also an Education. And he plays eminently fair when he offers Lismahago as Scotland embodied: dry, shrewd, brainy, contentious, brave, tough, reluctantly humorous, an "indefatigable economist" but not mean, a sound heart in a knotty casing.

The engraftment of the Scottish material is a true one, and the blood stream of the novel runs through it. The familial theme, for example, functions in it in a large and handsome way. At the Saturnalia of the Edinburgh cawdies, or street-runners, Cawdie Fraser addresses a toast to Jery: " 'Meester Malford, . . . may a' unkindness cease betwixt John Bull and his sister Moggy.' " Smollett turns the sibling relationship romantic in the ripening toward marriage of the robust affair of Tabby and Lismahago. Watching it ripen, Matthew Bramble muses, ". . . sure, if it produces any fruit, it must be of a very peculiar flavour." Of the particular marriage we anticipate no fruit, but of the political and social union we expect fruit peculiar but tart and invigorating. Another racy pairing is drawing closer, that of Humphry Clinker and Win Jenkins. And we feel Matthew Bramble drawing his whole little circle closer about him, with a warmth and trust increasingly familial.

The theme of improving health also accompanies the slowed action through Scotland. We sense a better color in the face, new strength in the gait, a general settling of nerves. By July 18 Matthew Bramble can write, "I now begin to feel the good effects of exercise—I eat like a farmer, sleep from mid-night till eight in the morning without interruption, and enjoy a constant tide of spirits, equally distant from inanition and excess." Win Jenkins reports of her mistress in Glasgow in early September, ". . . she ails nothing.—Her stomick is good, and she improves in grease and godliness. . . ." With the altar actually in view at last, even Tabby's spiteful temper seems somewhat mollified. Liddy is still subject to occasional flutters which require the goat's-whey cure, but she quickly comes round. She shows a quite new, more adult sharpness of view, at once penetrating and forbearing. Scotland "being exceedingly romantic, suits my turn and inclinations," she remarks; but then goes on to shrewd observations of her companions. "As for Mrs. Jenkins, she herself is really an object of compassion—Between vanity, methodism, and love, her head is almost turned." "My poor aunt, without any regard to her years and imperfections, has gone to market with her charms in every place where she thought she had the least chance to dispose of her person, which, however, hangs still heavy on her hands." By September 20, from Buxton, Matthew Bramble's references to his health, formerly his first and longest thought, are reduced to a laconic phrase in a postscript: "I . . . had no occasion for the water. . . ."

In the fourth and final movement of the novel, after the matter of Bath, the matter of London, and the matter of Scotland, the travelers set out upon a desultory course homeward, advancing "by slow steps towards the borders of Monmouthshire." The movement shudders, arrests, and then moves on to fulfill itself with a new inner energy in the events which follow Matthew Bramble's bare escape from drowning when the carriage overturns in a flooded stream. The consternation and then the relief of the whole party at his danger and his recovery form the most moving matter of the entire story. The perfect naturalness with which these extremes of feeling strike upon the reader testifies to the quiet massiveness with which Smollett has imposed his great simple hero. Not least impressive is the unembarrassed trepidation with which Jery writes the story to his Oxford friend:

> . . . I now sit down with a heart so full that it cannot contain itself; though I am under such agitation of spirits that you are to expect neither method nor connexion in this address—We have been this day within a hair's breadth of losing honest Matthew Bramble. . . .

When his beloved master, whom he has rescued, is finally brought to life at the inn, Humphry Clinker "laughed, and wept, and danced about in such a distracted manner, that the landlord very judiciously conveyed him out of the room." And Liddy, forgetting at long last all her maidenly mannerisms and behaving with sweet distraction, "ran thither half naked, with the wildest expression of eagerness in her countenance—Seeing the 'squire sitting up in the bed, she sprung forwards, and, throwing her arms about his neck, exclaimed in a most pathetic tone, 'Are you—Are you indeed my uncle— My dear uncle!—My best friend! My father!' "

The litany of terms with which Smollett supplies her— uncle, friend, father—is far from accidental or hysterical. Old Squaretoes, who on September 30 had still been thanking heaven "that among all the follies and weaknesses of human nature, I have not yet fallen into that of matrimony," finds himself on October 6 the firmly elected parent of the children of his dead sister. Now it transpires that he has long been a father in the flesh. Unbeknownst to him, Dorothy Twyford, "heretofore bar-keeper at the Angel at Chippenham," had borne him a son: Humphry Clinker "proves to be a crab of my own planting in the days of hot blood and unrestrained libertinism." Now the discoveries and the consequent matings and pairings, familial or quasi-familial, thicken apace: ". . . if it wance comes to marrying," as Win Jenkins says, "who nose but the frolick may go round." Mr. Bramble's party are rescued from the inn to the hospitality of a neighboring squire,

Charles Dennison, who proves to be his dear friend from university days. Dennison's young son George turns out to be the stroller Wilson, who has been pursuing Liddy about the country with such hopelessness that he has been made dangerously ill. His engagement to Liddy is quickly approved. Win Jenkins suffers an uneasy interval after the elevation of her lover Clinker, "matthew-murphy'd" into the son of the squire, but it is determined that their affair shall be allowed to go forward. So, as Win puts it in her lofty final epistle, there will be, with Tabitha and Lismahago, "three kiple chined, by the grease of God, in the holy bands of mattermoney."

Jery shakes his newly identified cousin Humphry Clinker "heartily by the hand." When he discovers his sister's lover is not the "wretched stroller" Wilson, whose life he has twice sought in duels, but "a gentleman, her equal in rank and superior in fortune," and, in the standard eighteenth-century form, "one of the most accomplished young fellows in England," he "rushed into his embrace, and they hugged one another as if they had been friends from infancy." In the handshake and the embrace as in the duels the potency of English class structure is being dramatized without apology. Smollett's real concern is to show Jery's warmth of heart and his joy in the accumulation of his family. His intolerance and his boyish precipitancy have been corrected before our eyes by time and experience, and he pronounces his own confession: "I am, however, mortified to reflect what flagrant injustice we every day commit, and what absurd judgment we form, in viewing objects through the falsifying medium of prejudice and passion."

Liddy's continuing maturity shows now in a kind of tense reconciliation to the rightness of forms that quite naturally needs time for confirmation. Equally naturally, being young and fearful and much tried, she is under an intense trepidation of spirits:

> I wish there may not be something treacherous in this sudden reconciliation of fortune—I have no merit—I have no title to such felicity! Far from enjoying the prospect that lies before me, my mind is harassed with a continued tumult, made up of hopes and wishes, doubts and apprehensions—I can neither eat nor sleep, and my spirits are in perpetual flutter.

For the first time she is trying and valuing the felicity of a passion blessed by a solid social and familial investment: "Wilson and I are now lodged in the same house, and converse together freely—His father approves of his sentiments in my favour; his mother loves me with all the tenderness of a parent; my uncle, my aunt, and my brother no longer oppose my inclinations." We watch her achieving an adjustment to decorum unconsciously right: she feels forms not as ends in themselves but as useful small ceremonials, signs of and means to dignity, which is a sign of and a means to orderly human intercourse and calm of mind. How much more decorum and how much more real content, as compared to modern forms of the phrase, are expressed in her invitation to Letty to attend her in her approaching wedding: "I must beg you will come and do the last offices of maidenhood to your companion Lydia Melford." For her maturity is a matter of language, too, visible in the precision, the grave cordiality, of her directions for the journey:

> The distance from hence to Gloucester, does not exceed one hundred miles, and the roads are good.—Mr. Clinker, alias Loyd, shall be sent over to attend your motions—If you step into the post-chaise, with your maid Betty Barker, at seven in the morning, you will arrive by four in the afternoon at the half-way house, where there is good accommodation. There you shall be met by my brother and myself, who will next day conduct you to this place, where, I am sure, you will find yourself perfectly at your ease in the midst of an agreeable society.

Her note to her "worthy governess" in Gloucester, pleading for the favor of Letty's company in this "interesting crisis," is an absolute paradigm of its kind, phrased with warm appeal, quiet contrition, and modest satisfaction.

Measured forms are shaping the daily as well as the future life. The gentlemen "went a-shooting yesterday, and made a great havock among the partridges"; tomorrow they will "take field against the woodcocks and snipes." Evenings they "dance and sing, or play at commerce, loo, and quadrille; shortly they are "resolved to convert the great hall into a theatre, and get up the *Beaux Stratagem* without delay." The action is assuming the geometrical and terpsichorean shapes so dear to the eighteenth century, so classic to comedy, so basic to the agreeable conduct of life. Jery as well as Matthew Bramble sees the humorousness that accompanies the shapeliness of the new order: "this country dance," he calls it; and, inclusively, "the comedy." The long winnowing action of the Expedition is completing itself in a final clear and symmetrical sorting and settling, onto a plane of reason, health, and affection "equally distant," in the phrase of Mr. Bramble's earlier letter, "from inanition and excess."

In the general autumn-evening glow of the novel's close, Jery finds that "the vinegar of Mrs. Tabby is remarkably dulcified," and that the temper of Lismahago, "which had been soured and shrivelled by disappointment and chagrin, is now swelled out, and smoothed like a raisin in plum-porridge." The temper of honest Matthew Bramble is no longer even in question. He is the smiling center of a circle of happiness, well because he is happy and happy because he is well. He has found in Charles Dennison's country estate "that pitch of rural felicity, at which I have been aspiring these twenty years in vain," and his own inward peace is now so settled and undemanding that he can for the time take his "axercise" *in situ*, like Chowder in his post-chaise, working actively from the inside out, in a "vigorous circulation of the spirits, which is the very essence and criterion of good health." He has health to spare for others now, and he moves to rescue his old friend Baynard, reduced to indigence, illness, and almost to imbecility by a vain and tyrannical wife who has at last found the grace to die. He designs a sweeping reorganization of Baynard's agrarian and spiritual economy.

In Mr. Bramble's last letter the young folk are for Bath, but Lieutenant Lismahago and his lady, and Mr. Bramble and his new acquist, will take leave of them at Gloucester, where the wonderful business so inauspiciously began, and make for Brambleton-hall, where Dr. Lewis is desired to "prepare a good chine and turkey for our Christmas dinner." Dinner will be shared by Baynard, whose spirits he will watch over until the spring. "In less than a year, I make no doubt, but he will find himself perfectly at ease both in his mind and body, for the one had dangerously affected the other; and I shall enjoy the exquisite pleasure of seeing my friend rescued from misery and contempt." Mr. Bramble is determined to "take the heath in all weathers," and to "renounce all sedentary amusements, particularly that of writing long letters."

But without the letters of Smollett's little troupe of originals, with their sweetly reverberatory treatment of shared experience, their caressing and crotchety over-and-overing of events, their marvelous readiness, fullness, and purity of response, his correspondents for two hundred years would have been the poorer.

Sterne and the Absurd
Homunculus

RT is art because it is not life,' but art is useful because it is of life. Art is 'but a vision of reality,' Yeats said. It matters both that its mode is visionary, a record of illuminated and perhaps systematic insight, and that it treats of the real as knowable: what it looks at is life as experienced. All art deals in its way, however forthright or elliptical, with the race of man and his life in time. In this grand abstract sense, all art is metaphor, not life itself but tropes, significant imaginative forms of life. 'All metaphor, Malachi, stilts and all,' Yeats exclaims in "High Talk." Experience has always offered as the life of man to the vision of art the same fundamental disastrous landscape with figures. It needs no Smelfungus, as Sterne wickedly called Smollett, to admit that even the fortunate races have defined life between Eden and the Hereafter as basically tragic. Our joys we understand as small secular miracles lightening the painful way to the dark: 'Golden lads and girls all must, As chimney-sweepers, come to dust.' Art is serious not as an end in itself but as a means to speech in our 'affair with the gods,' a vocabulary in which we talk to them, in praise and protest. Art need not be sad to be serious: laughter may be serviceable and thereby serious. A comic masterpiece such as *The Life and Opinions of Tristram Shandy, Gent.* may be as fully occupied as more patently serious works in conducting the affair with the gods. That it is so occupied has something to do with its being a masterpiece.

At the end of the *Symposium*, that least Platonic and most Shandean of the dialogues, so grand at the center and so bacchanalian about the edges, Socrates speaks in a tantalizing and paradoxical way of an idea we should like to understand better. In the course of a long night, love has been defined, deified, and mocked, and the bottomless Socrates, with his infinite capacity to take and to give, to talk and to drink, retains the only unfuddled head among the banqueters; in a dawn made hazy by drink, exhaustion, and high talk, Aristodemus takes in the idea but sleepily:

> . . . the chief thing which he remembered was Socrates compelling the other two to acknowledge that the genius of comedy was the same with that of tragedy, and that the true artist in tragedy was an artist in comedy also. To this they were constrained to assent, being drowsy, and not quite following the argument.

Like Aristodemus, we "did not hear the beginning of the discourse"; we feel a bit fuddled, and we don't follow the argument. Plato means apparently that the genius of the two main dramatic modes ought to be interchangeable, not that the modes themselves are indistinct. Still, even if we agree that a writer of genius will possess both powers, we conclude that he chooses to write comedy rather than tragedy by an act of will rising out of a cast of temperament. Tragedy and comedy are not one thing; the distinction is real, an either-or, and a useful one. Though he nearly breaks our hearts in his progress, even Chekhov finally convinces us that he is writing comedy. Shakespeare ravishes us with a variety of comic delights on his way to unmistakably tragic destinations. Gulley Jimson laughs in order to hold off the paralysis of the creative will that comes from "getting up a grievance" with a brutal world; he is racked by laughter, and he dies laughing. "Same thing, mother," he assures the nursing nun in his last ambulance when she advises him to pray rather than giggle. "Such a waggish leering as lurks in all your horribles," says Stubb in

Moby Dick. The surviving Greek tragedies seem almost totally humorless; yet there is the baffling and suggestive phenomenon of the satyr play which was regularly offered at the end of the early trilogies. To say that tragedy and comedy are different is not to say that they are unrelated. One need not blur a true distinction to see that as each goes about its proper business they meet often in a mysterious and fruitful marriage from which they proceed not confused but complicated and enriched.

That interfertilization may be as well worth study as the sufficiently difficult business of defining the two genres. Tragedy and comedy share a vision of ironic incongruity in representative experience. Both present particulars from which we generalize if we choose. Tragedy treats of the hiatus between the ideal and the real, the loss of the perfect. Comedy enjoys the gap between the normal and the abnormal, the ordinary and the hyperbolic; in Aristotle's and Fielding's word, its subject is the "ridiculous." Both genres I suppose are swellings, modes of exaggeration: tragedy presenting man's heightened erroneousness, the lamentably grand in him; comedy his heightened pretense and delusion, the laughably absurd. Both finally bring him low before the gods, before his kind, and before his dream of himself. *Tristram Shandy* seems to me an example of the kind of high art, seriously unsad, that a writer of genius may make from the standard disastrous landscape, resolving by an act of will and temperament to declare it comic.

An attempt to derive Sterne's character from his writings, dangerous by definition, fails in practice. The felt presence of the man in the work is shifting and slippery. Just when you think you have him the real man, or his representative in the narrative, goes capering off to Dover or Flanders and leaves you holding some rag of his costume. Sterne's is a personality that would be unthinkable in the American Protestant church;

in the English church it is merely astonishing. We do not know his life in really satisfactory detail. We sense in his Parson Yorick an embodiment of Sterne's understanding of the graver side of his own nature, penetrating, pitiful, witty, "Cervantick," gaily acerb. But it was Sterne after all who chose to call his parson Yorick and to trace his lineage back to a certain Danish original who was a fellow of infinite jest, wont to set the table on a roar. The narrator of *Tristram Shandy*, however, is not this Yorick, or the softer Yorick of *A Sentimental Journey*, but another, stranger creature called Tristram, and the theatre of the comedy is this new jester's brilliantly disordered cranial chamber.

We wish we could be surer about how the persona is related to the writer, for that would let us be clearer on the purpose behind it all, and would lead us closer to the mysterious and fascinating character of "the man Sterne," as Dr. Johnson called him, in High Church contempt. We do know that Sterne was a chronic consumptive, one who might have spoken like Pope of "this long disease, my life." His "leaky bellows" failed him for the first time as he was about to leave Cambridge, and there he bled his first "bed full," as he liked to put it, the first of many before the final sufficient one in 1768. Sterne knew most of his adult life that he was a dying man. Something we can learn of his relationship to Tristram by watching how Tristram treats the data of his own sickness in the narrative. In the whole of the long volume there are no more than half a dozen references to Tristram's own fragile health. He speaks of "these two spider legs of mine," and several times of his "cough" or his "asthma."

> To this hour art thou not tormented with the vile asthma thou gattest in skating against the wind in Flanders? and is it but two months ago, that in a fit of laughter, on seeing a cardinal make water like a quirister (with both hands) thou brakest a vessel in thy lungs, whereby, in two hours, thou lost as many

quarts of blood; and hadst thou lost as much more, did not the faculty tell thee—it would have amounted to a gallon?

. . . And so, with this moral for the present, may it please your worships and your reverences, I take my leave of you till this time twelve-month, when, (unless this vile cough kills me in the mean time) I'll have another pluck at your beards, and lay open a story to the world you little dream of.

Such is his ordinary happy way of managing the matter. The one feeling and forthright apostrophe to the blessing of health is situated in an absurd little chapter treating of Walter Shandy's hobby-horsical fascination with "the due contention for mastery betwixt the radical heat and the radical moisture." Though Sterne's full manner cannot be clear without larger context, it is obvious that he does not exploit the legitimate theme of illness, or even give it anything like due realistic weight. Every reference is in fact turned from its own nature and made to serve another end; each is understated and under-cut, and thereby trimmed for insertion into the larger design, the comic fabric.

This is one way of seeing that Tristram is a highly arti-ficial creature, and stands at the center of a web of artifice. The point is not that ill health is unreal or unserious, but that such mannered behavior is one way of dealing with an ex-perience that is only too insupportably real and common. Tris-tram embodies for his creator a mode of deportment, chosen by an act of will and of temperament, which aims to convey and control the anarchy of experience by travestying it in a formalized exaggeration. At first glance *Tristram Shandy* seems one of the maddest books ever written, and Sterne de-lights to abet that impression of "this rhapsodical work," as he calls it, proclaiming his amateurishness ("I am but just set up in the business, so know little about it"), assuring us that he is governed by his pen, that he puts down one word and "trusts to God Almighty for the next," and so on. Of course all this is part of the studious method in the madness. The

Lockeian psychology of association of ideas is always strongly but flexibly at work, the study of "duration and its simple modes" really is going on. But the governing order is the controlled disorder of a gay and serious mind luxuriously at play. The mind is Sterne's, transmuted as Tristram's. The madness has purpose as well as method, and the interesting thing to consider is the relationship of means and ends.

If the world of the book is the theatre of the mind of Tristram, then it is the histrionic thing that Sterne's intelligence chooses to make of the world of real experience by transmitting and transmuting it through the sensibility of his special creature Tristram. "I write a careless kind of a civil, nonsensical, good humoured *Shandean* book," Tristram says, "which will do all your hearts good." Being Shandean the book is *sui generis*, as Sterne knows and intends. The book itself must tell us what and why is Shandeism. Its salutes to Rabelais and especially to Cervantes are of help, for they indicate the lineage Sterne wishes to claim. Like Aristotle, Sterne likes his medical metaphor, and he frequently describes his purpose in anatomical terms:

> True *Shandeism*, think what you will against it, opens the heart and lungs, and like all those affections which partake of its nature, it forces the blood and other vital fluids of the body to run freely through its channels, and makes the wheel of life run long and cheerfully round. . . .

> If 'tis wrote against any thing,—'tis wrote, an' please your worships, against the spleen; in order, by a more frequent and more convulsive elevation and depression of the diaphragm, and the succussations of the intercostal and abdominal muscles in laughter, to drive the *gall* and other *bitter juices* from the gall bladder, liver and sweet-bread of his majesty's subjects, with all the inimicitious passions which belong to them, down into their duodenums.

The book then is an Anatomy of Hilarity. If the bitter juices can be driven down into the duodenums of his majesty's subjects, presumably they are in a fair way to be purged. Clearly that is what Shandeism is aiming at: it is a bolus of laughter, a specific calculated to cleanse and sweeten a bitter condition. Goethe wrote of Sterne, "Whoever reads him feels himself lifted above the petty cares of the world. His humour is inimitable, and it is not every kind of humour that leaves the soul calm and serene." His is the purgative effect of great art of any kind. For comedy offers its catharsis too, nor is it immune to pity and fear, in less radical forms of the massive emotions of tragedy.

". . . Yet have I carried myself towards thee in such fanciful guise of careless disport," Tristram says to the reader, and it is easy to suppose the theatre of his mind a mere disorderly cockpit, wholly given over to frivolous doings—so vivid is the farce-comedy of wild invention and analogy, of bawdry and buffoonery. Sterne seems so to interpret his own mind in a letter to his friend John Hall-Stevenson:

> . . . I have not managed my miseries like a wise man—and if God, for my consolation under them, had not poured forth the spirit of Shandeism into me, which will not suffer me to think two moments upon any grave subject, I would else, just now, lay down and die—die—.

But his image in a letter of the same period to David Garrick seems to me nearer the truth:

> I laugh 'till I cry, and in the same tender moments *cry 'till I laugh*. I Shandy it more than ever, and verily do believe, that by mere Shandeism sublimated by a laughter-loving people, I fence as much against infirmities, as I do by the benefit of air and climate.

Shandeism is in fact a pose—a stance, an attitude, a particular histrionic inclination of mind, body, and the facial muscles. But the pose rises out of a serious purpose. "Fence" is Sterne's operative word here. The pose of Shandeism is a fence of wit, and it is called for because there are terrible things in the landscapes which must be contained, that they may not overrun us.

In one of his rare obviously serious moments, dedicating to Pitt the second edition of the first two volumes of Tristram Shandy, Sterne uses the same figure:

> . . . I live in a constant endeavor to fence against the infirmities of ill health, and other evils of life, by mirth; being firmly persuaded that every time a man smiles,—but much more so, when he laughs, that it adds something to this Fragment of Life.

In his more habitual way, his vision of the terrible is rendered as comedy, it is undercut and derided. When he speaks of "this scurvy and disastrous world of ours . . . this vile, dirty planet of ours,—which, 'o my conscience, . . . I take to be made up of the shreds and clippings of the rest . . . one of the vilest worlds that ever was made," he is scoffing at and through his own hyperbole. Similarly, the incongruous detail, the style of direct address, and the gusty tone make loud mock of a lamentable catalogue of disaster:

> What a jovial and merry world would this be, may it please your worships, but for that inextricable labyrinth of debts, cares, woes, want, grief, discontent, melancholy, large jointures, impositions, and lies!

The wit-fence confines the terrible within the region of laughter, that it may not irrupt into the region of tears. The fence does not obliterate the terrors; it is of open mesh and they show through, but they are held on the other side, where they may be lived with.

The Shandean pose behind the method of narration directs the weaving of the book's web of artifice. The coordinating metaphor, I think, is the traditional one of the life of man conceived as a journey, which we know so omnipresently in literature. Sterne wrenches and disjoins the journey, scatters the fragments not quite helter-skelter, but the traditional motive is always there and always important. The journey metaphor is natively so haunting to our minds that the traveler and his fate always take on the force of racial or representative experience. The innate richness of the motive is not denied to comedy: consider *Don Quixote* or *Joseph Andrews* or *Huckleberry Finn*. In Sterne's comedy the principal traveler is Tristram. We follow him from the cradle not quite to the grave (several times we find him capering on the grave's edge). In fact we follow him *ab ovo*, as he cheerfully points out. We meet him first at the moment of generation, as the Homunculus, "so young a traveller, my little gentleman," sent on his way, radically confused by Mrs. Shandy's untimely question about the clock, to address the egg. Thenceforward the absurd Homunculus, the mannikin who is man, inhabits this Life and Opinions as racial representative, the disheveled champion of an archetype of the life of man defined as comedy. His father Walter Shandy, with his hobby-horsical fixation on the homeopathy of the procreative act, mourns that disastrous moment

> when the few animal spirits I was worth in the world, and with which memory, fancy, and quick parts should have been conveyed,—were all dispersed, confused, confounded, scattered, and sent to the devil.

This is only the beginning. Tristram meets misfortune in "my geniture, nose, and name," in all the events Walter Shandy sees as crucial to the destiny of the child: ". . . this *Tristram* of ours, I find, comes very hardly by all his religious rites." In a sub-chapter formally entitled "My Father's Lamentation," Mr. Shandy turns the process into an oration:

> Unhappy *Tristram*! child of wrath! child of decrepitude! interruption! mistake! and discontent! What one misfortune or disaster in the book of embryotic evils, that could unmechanize thy frame, or entangle thy filaments! which has not fallen upon thy head, or ever thou camest into the world—what evils in thy passage into it!—what evils since! . . . .

And Tristram says in his own plaintive pipe,

> . . . in every stage of my life, and at every turn and corner

where she could get fairly at me, the ungracious Duchess [Fortune] has pelted me with a set of as pitiful misadventures and cross accidents as ever small Hero sustained.

The smallness of the hero, the wilful reduction of the representative man, suggests the point of his function. By progressive insult from chance and unworthy instruments, he is stripped of dignity as well as size. His geniture is spoiled by Mrs. Shandy's bovine thoughtlessness; his nose is smashed by an inept *accoucheur*; half his name is lost because a foolish chambermaid cannot carry the whole and his father cannot find his trousers in time; then, when he persists in struggling on toward manhood, he suffers a near-castration from a sash-window the weights of which have been plundered to make cannon in a backyard game of war. "I'll put him, however, into breeches, said my father,—let the world say what it will," Tristram reports in a sentence that is called a chapter. In a sense the image becomes a trope for the whole history; the standard ludicrousness of the Homunculus who is man, inadequate to the event which is life, perpetually too small for his costume.

We realize at last that Sterne has conceived all his people, not only Tristram, as Homunculi. In the general histrionic enterprise the master puppeteer Sterne manipulates his puppet-puppeteer Tristram, who manipulates a little troupe of puppet-originals who mime the absurdity of the race in its standard forms. All of them are busy salvaging comedy for us out of the mischance of their lives. Each of Tristram's catastrophes is a unit in the destruction of his father's dream of his son. And Walter Shandy's luxuriant intellectualism, his terrific flux of words and ideas, his discovery of a "North west passage to the intellectual world" by way of the auxiliary verbs, do not help him to oil the hinge of the parlor door, to stub up his ox moor, or to find his trousers in time to prevent the misnaming of his son. Mrs. Shandy's invincible calm, her perpetual unsurprise, do not keep the world from seeing that her serenity is stupidity. The grotesque mismatching of husband and wife is a type of the standard mismatching of human relationships:

> Cursed luck!—said he to himself, . . . for a man to be master of one of the finest chains of reasoning in nature,—and have a wife at the same time with such a head-piece, that he cannot hang up a single inference within side of it, to save his soul from destruction.

The mismatching of the brothers Shandy speaks to the same purpose. Doctor Slop, "great son of *Pilumnus*," arrives at Mrs. Shandy's confinement in majesty of mud, slashes his thumb in trying to deliver his instruments from the green bays bag that Obadiah has tied in twenty hard knots, is forced to sit through a long derision of his Catholicism, lacerates Uncle Toby's knuckles in demonstrating his new-invented forceps, and finally makes a shambles of Tristram's birth. Until they are betrayed by the Peace of Utrecht, Uncle Toby with his wound upon the groin and Corporal Trim with his wound upon the knee stagger through the absurdity of their mannikin wars on the bowling green. When we watch Toby limping off between a crutch and a lame corporal from his brother's house in the city to mount his hobby-horse in the country, we feel we have been granted an image of the whole tragicomedy of man in life.

The Homunculus, Tristram says, is "as much and as truly our fellowcreature as my Lord Chancellor of England." Sterne's comic treatment of character makes the statement reversible: we are all Homunculi as absurd as Tristram Shandy. That is the reason for the elaboration and interconnection of the modes of artifice in the novel, the logic of its illogic. Sterne discovered the absurd two centuries before the moderns, and understood it not less philosophically. His recourse is laughter and, "in the same tender moments," tears, complicated in special ways. *Tristram Shandy* is the absurd made comically programmatic. The formalizing of the artifice conduces both to comedy and to philosophical statement. By so intricately manipulating the anarchy of experience, Sterne asserts a tyrannizing control that at once renders the absurd laughable and declares it representative, philosophically normative. Thus the detailed theatricality of Sterne's method: Tristram's posturing narrative stance and his jester's cap and bells; his jocular manner of address to a putative "sir" or "madam," like stage talk or drawing room *conversazione*; his cinematographic conduct of the flights of his associational imagination, seemingly whimsical and wild, actually schematically patterned; all the minutiae of attention to tones of voice and to costume and to attitudes of body.

Insisting on his frivolousness, Sterne creates a hectic disunity of surface and a special brazen tonality as his jester's standard mode of address. Sterne's page is orchestrated almost like a sheet of music. His most obvious means are graphic or typographic. He litters his page with italics, dashes, exclamation points, asterisks, and lacunae, and further complicates the texture to the eye by bold face and black letter type, long passages in French or Latin, absurd nomenclature, burlesque footnotes. He gives us a blank page, a black page, and a marbled page, and draws out for the eye the madly convoluted "line" of his plot. He "omits" one chapter entirely. He pauses after he is under way to compose a sort of all-purpose dedication, "a true Virgin-Dedication untried on," which he then offers to sell to "any one Duke, Marquis, Earl, Viscount, or Baron, in these his Majesty's dominions, who stands in need of a tight, genteel dedication. . . ." It is "much at his service for fifty guineas," Tristram says. A third of the way through the book he pauses again to compose a preface, supplies the heading, then abandons the whole idea. But the most interesting of Sterne's typographical tricks is his occasional reduction of a scene or a story to a kind of quick shorthand image, a diagrammatic chart. Thus Walter Shandy and his brother

Toby shake their heads in unison at the phenomenon of the added dignity that comes to all the females in a house of child-birth; Toby shakes in humility and admiration, Walter in amused exasperation:

> ... from the very moment the mistress of the house is brought to bed, every female in it, from my lady's gentlewoman down to the cinder-wench, becomes an inch taller for it; and give themselves more airs upon that single inch, than all the other inches put together.
>
> I think rather, replied my uncle *Toby*, that 'tis we who sink an inch lower.—If I but meet a woman with child—I do it— 'Tis a heavy tax upon that half of our fellow-creatures, brother *Shandy*, said my uncle *Toby*, . . . shaking his head.—Yes, yes, 'tis a painful thing—said my father, shaking his head too—but certainly since shaking of heads came into fashion, never did two heads shake together, in concert, from two such different springs.
>
> God bless ⎫ 'em all—said my uncle *Toby* and my
> Deuce take ⎭   father, each to himself.

Or the delicious chart-story of Amandus and Amanda, "two fond lovers, separated from each other by cruel parents, and by still more cruel destiny":

> Amandus—He
> Amanda—She—

each ignorant of the other's course,

> He—east
> She—west

Amandus taken captive by the Turks, and carried to the emperor of Morocco's court, where the princess of Morocco falling in love with him, keeps him twenty years in prison for the love of his Amanda.—
She—(Amanda) all the time wandering barefoot, and with dishevelled hair, o'er rocks and mountains, enquiring for Amandus!—Amandus! Amandus!—making every hill and valley to echo back his name—

> Amandus! Amandus!

at every town and city, sitting down forlorn at the gate—Has Amandus!—has my Amandus entered? —till, going round, and round, and round the world—chance unexpected bringing them at the same moment of the night, though by different ways, to the gate of Lyons their native city, and each in well known accents calling out aloud,

> Is my Amandus ⎫
> Is my Amanda ⎭ still alive?

they fly into each other's arms, and both drop down dead for joy.

Sterne's management of the device makes graphic, and thus usefully plain, what he is doing in subtler ways throughout the book. He is presenting real patterns with exaggerated emphasis, stage-managing comic-pathetic archetypes of experience, burlesque extensions of ordinary disasters, conducting the Homunculus in all his forms through the absurd dance of life.

Sterne is pleased to protest what is obviously untrue, that the pace and direction of his narrative movement are whimsical and unplanned. He marvels, for example, at his own profligacy in spending two chapters to conduct the brothers Shandy down one flight of stairs: ". . . we are got no farther yet than to the first landing, and there are fifteen more steps down to the bottom; and for aught I know, as my father and my uncle *Toby* are in a talking humour, there may be as many chapters as steps. . . ." His defense of his digressive movement is nearer the mark. After admiring one of his by-flights as "a masterstroke of digressive skill," he goes on to point out that yet "I constantly take care to order affairs so, that my main business does not stand still in my absence." An analysis of Uncle Toby's character has been interrupted by the affair of Aunt Dinah and her coachman and by still wilder matters, yet "the drawing of my uncle *Toby's* character went on gently all the time." Thus, Tristram says, "my work is digressive, and it is progressive too,—and at the same time." His summary makes use of a significant figure:

> ... I have constructed the main work and the adventitious parts
> of it with intersections, and have so complicated and involved
> the digressive and progressive movements, one wheel within
> another, that the whole machine, in general, has been kept
> a-going;—and, what's more, shall be kept a-going these forty
> years, if it pleases the fountain of health to bless me so long
> with life and good spirits.

Though the whole argument is designed to appear specious
and playful, it largely speaks truth. The main business of the
novel, in so far as the adventures of the Shandy family are
the main business, rarely stands stockstill. And in the larger
comic sense in which the adventures of the absurd Homunculus
are the main business, that business never rests for an instant;
it is as pointedly active in the digressions as in the progressions.

But Sterne's argument is less important in itself than the
attitudinizing with which it is conducted. There is a self-consciousness, a sort of dandyism, about it which can lead us toward the center of his comic method. What Sterne gives us
is not only an art about life, but an art about an art about life.
It is always aware of itself, always aware of its own awareness, and constantly jogging us to pay attention to these aware-
nesses. Sterne's dwelling upon minutiae of attitude and modulation is a part of this systematic comic self-consciousness; as
Tristram puts it, "Attitudes are nothing, madam—'tis the
transition from one attitude to another—like the preparation
and resolution of the discord into harmony, which is all in all."
We feel it also in language. When Sterne speaks of the "machinery" or "the whole machine" of his work, his affair of
whirling concentric wheels, we are being asked to see a con-
traption of deliberate artifice, that aims to speak as much
through its patterned mechanism of movement as through the
material of character and action which it is turning in order
to shape. The method self-mockingly reduces itself before
our eyes to an affair of manipulation and management, a
game, and a game of skill: "All the dexterity," Tristram says,
"is in the good cookery and management. . . ." The machine

is an absurd one, but it knows its own absurdity, and chooses it as appropriate to its object and subject, the absurd Homunculus. We can observe the dandyism at work, its constant awareness of self, subject, audience, and manner, as it observes itself observing a single brief scene, the "two orators" Corporal Trim and Walter Shandy, about to perform on the occasion of the death of Tristram's older brother Bobby, a "lad of wonderful slow parts" who never directly appears in the novel. At the same time we can recall that the machine of wit is not essentially egoistic or heartless, and that the self-awareness is clinical and ironic:

> A curious observer of nature, had he been worth the inventory of all Job's stock . . . would have given the half of it, to have heard corporal *Trim* and my father, two orators so contrasted by nature and education, haranguing over the same bier.
> My father a man of deep reading—prompt memory—with *Cato*, and *Seneca*, and *Epictetus*, at his finger's ends.—
> The corporal—with nothing—to remember—of no deeper reading than his muster-roll—or greater names at his finger's end, than the contents of it.
> The one proceeding from period to period, by metaphor and allusion, and striking the fancy as he went along, (as men of wit and fancy do) with the entertainment and pleasantry of his pictures and images.
> The other, without wit or antithesis, or point, or turn, this way or that; but leaving the images on one side, and the pictures on the other, going straight forwards as nature could lead him, to the heart. O *Trim*! would to heaven thou hadst a better historian!—would!—thy historian had a better pair of breeches!—O ye critics! will nothing melt you?

Sterne is charmed and moved by his subject here, and so his language is precise, direct, inartificial. Elsewhere this is not commonly the case: the language is habitually full of histrionic pretense, a fundamental part of the machinery of jest. Sterne uses ancient devices of language, familiar from Burton and Swift and Rabelais and Cervantes, with a genial energy and robustiousness that makes them new again. His pleasure and ours comes from the separate acts of word play, the local excitement each makes on the page, and from the accumulating harmony of the language at work with the larger comic design, a brilliant sorting of means to ends. Again, by his way of using words, Sterne is constantly calling attention to the fact of his artifice and its service in the anti-heroic history of the Homunculus who is man. Of course this congruity is often formed by incongruity, an inappropriateness of the size of terms to the apparent size of the issue, which generally aims to shrink the issue to its proper ridiculousness. So Tristram supplies, to account for his birth at home rather than in London, a hilarious document of nearly three pages, a burlesque of legal cant (thus a travesty of a travesty of language), stipulating in his mother's marriage settlement that she is to be allowed to bear her children in London unless she forfeits the right to one turn by causing the preceding journey to be made "upon false cries and tokens":

> . . . for the well and truly hiring of one coach, with able and sufficient horses, to carry and convey the body of the said *Elizabeth Mollineux*, and the child or children which she shall be then and there enceint and pregnant with,—unto the city of *London*. . . . and have free ingress, egress, and regress throughout her journey, in and from the said coach, according to the tenor, true intent, and meaning of these presents, without any let, suit, trouble, disturbance, molestation, discharge, hindrance, forfeiture, eviction, vexation, interruption, or incumbrance whatsoever.

And so on. "In three words," Tristram drily sums up, "my mother was to lay in, (if she chose it) in *London*."

Mock-heroic language ridicules Dr. Slop's pretentious professionalism and pseudo-science:

> Truce!—truce, good Dr. *Slop*!—stay thy obstetric hand. . . . Besides, great son of *Pilumnus*! What canst thou do? — Thou hast come forth unarmed;—thou hast left thy *tire-tête*. —thy new-invented *forceps*,—thy *crotchet*,—thy *squirt*, and all thy instruments of salvation and deliverance behind thee.—

By heaven! at this moment they are hanging up in a green bays bag, betwixt thy two pistols, at the bed's head!

Uncle Toby's mimic wars, already reduced to toys on a bowling green, are comically reinflated by the mouth-filling martial lingo with which he and Trim communicate so solemnly. Tristram puts an end to some of this nonsense with a nonsensical apostrophe to Toby; then abruptly ends his chapter in order, he says, "to let the apostrophe cool." Walter Shandy's fetish as to noses is sustained by the opinion of one *Ambrose Paraeus* that a child's nose is formed according to the quality of the nurse's breast: by a firm breast the nose is "so snubbed, so rebuffed, so rebated, and so refrigerated . . . as never to arrive *ad mensuram suam legitimam*," whereas by a soft breast, "by sinking into it . . . as into so much butter," the nose is "comforted, nourished, plumped up, refreshed, refocillated, and set a growing forever."

This returns us to the Homunculus as a specific image, and we find him repeatedly subjected to comic mistreatment by the vocabulary, the context, and the rhythm of the language. Here is Walter Shandy on the crucial subject of how the creature gets itself born:

> . . . the lax and pliable state of a child's head in parturition, the bones of the cranium having no sutures at that time, was such,—that by force of the woman's efforts, which, in strong labour-pains, was equal, upon an average, to the weight of 470 pounds avoirdupois acting perpendicularly upon it;—it so happened, that in 49 instances out of 50, the said head was compressed and moulded into the shape of an oblong conical piece of dough, such as a pastry-cook generally rolls up in order to make a pie of.—Good God! cried my father, what havoc and destruction must this make in the infinitely fine and tender texture of the cerebellum!—Or if there is such a juice as *Borri* pretends,—is it not enough to make the clearest liquor in the world both feculent and mothery?

Tristram's father characteristically makes his peace with the accidental circumcision of his son by the unweighted sash-window by turning to the subject in the books of ancient authors:

> . . . he rose up, and rubbing his forehead two or three times across with the palm of his hand, in the manner we rub out the footsteps of care, when evil has trod lighter upon us than we foreboded,—he shut the book, and walked down stairs.— Nay, said he, mentioning the name of a different great nation upon every step as he set his foot upon it—if the EGYPTIANS, —the SYRIANS,—the PHOENICIANS,—the ARABIANS,—the CAPADOCIANS,—if the COLCHI, and TROGLODYTES did it—if SOLON and PYTHAGORAS submitted,—what is TRISTRAM—Who am I, that I should fret or fume one moment about the matter? *

In fact Walter Shandy comes very close to living a life of language. He floats in a great flux of words—talk, reading, scribbling, speculating. Words are food and medicine to him. He is saved from entire ridiculousness by his "sub-acid" wit and his stout satirical alertness. But words are his hobby-horse, and Sterne makes it plain that when he is fairly mounted he is not far from mad. In the long run words do not save the Homunculus either. They are a recourse from absurdity and pain, but not an ultimate recourse; there really is no North-west passage to the intellectual world by way of the auxiliary verbs.

A glance back at the management of Walter Shandy's dis-course on accidental circumcision, each of his periods punc-tuated by the bounce of a foot on the stairs, will show the kind of thing Sterne does to the comic Homunculus by means of gesture and attitudes of body. In this important part of his puppetry he achieves most of his effects by a kind of micro-scopic attention to details of posture and movement, often rendering these minutiae in language incongruously over-blown. Tristram's congenital oddity of nature first betrays

---

* "Ilus, continued my father, circumcised his whole army one morn-ing.—Not without a court martial? cried my uncle *Toby*."

itself in childhood by "a most unaccountable obliquity . . . in my manner of setting up my top. . . ." Walter Shandy is horrified by the image rising out of the opinion of "*Coglionissimo Borri*, the great *Milanese* physician," that the *Animus* and the *Anima*, the two forms of the soul, float in a fragrant juice he has discovered in "the cellulae of the occipital parts of the cerebellum," "taking up her residence, and sitting dabbling, like a tadpole, all day long, both summer and winter, in a puddle. . . ." Tristram spends several chapters in extricating his father from the contortion that follows from reaching with his left hand across his body for his handkerchief in a pocket set low in the right-hand skirt of a long coat. Uncle Toby's whistling of *Lillabullero*, his habitual gentle substitute for satirical commentary on the ridiculous before his eyes, is described in this kind of detail:

> My Uncle *Toby* instantly withdrew his hand from off my father's knee, reclined his body gently back in his chair, raised his head till he could just see the cornice of the room, and then directing the buccinatory muscles along his cheeks, and the orbicular muscles around his lips to do their duty—he whistled *Lillabullero.*

But probably Sterne's most brilliant piece of comic attitudinizing is his picture of Walter Shandy's theatrical grief when he first hears of the ruination of Tristram's nose in birth. "Lead me, brother *Toby*, . . . to my room this instant," he cries, and staggers up the stairs. In his chamber,

> . . . he threw himself prostrate across his bed in the wildest disorder imaginable, but at the same time in the most lamentable attitude of a man borne down with sorrows, that ever the eye of pity dropped a tear for.—The palm of his right hand, as he fell upon the bed, receiving his forehead, and covering the greatest part of both his eyes, gently sunk down with his head (his elbow giving way backwards) till his nose touched the quilt;—his left arm hung insensible over the side of the bed, his knuckles reclining upon the handle of the chamber-pot, which peeped out beyond the valance,—his right leg (his left

being drawn up towards his body) hung half over the side of the bed, the edge of it pressing upon his shin-bone.—He felt it not. A fixed, inflexible sorrow took possession of every line of his face.—He sighed once,—heaved his breast often,—but uttered not a word.

That these various attitudes, Walter's exaggerated emotionalism, Trim's hortatory calisthenics, Toby's melting naiveté, are in part "attitudes" or assumed postures, and that they are habitual, is one key to Sterne's intention. Being habitual they are patterned, and weave directly into the larger comic pattern, the web of that artifice. Being tagged, customary, anticipated, specified to the person, they move in the open and angular way of stereotypes in the comic dance. The "machinery" of Sterne's wit works in this way, with the hyperbolic directness and candor, the absence of refinement and hesitation, a willingly assumed crudity, which is general to comedy. Sterne's special angle of vision, his oblique microscopy, is another key to meaning. It is the way an alert, loving, and satirical sensibility looks at creatures touching and laughable, in sum ridiculous. When Boswell marveled at his attention to small matters, Johnson replied gravely that nothing was too small for so small a creature as man. Sterne works through the same conviction, assumed comically without frivolity. The particularity of his scrutiny turns the Homunculus into a specimen, and distances and shrinks him into the toy that he is in proportion to the demands of his destiny. Very different in tone, Sterne's proportional mathematics are otherwise similar to Swift's in the second book of *Gulliver's Travels*. As his method is less obvious in consonance with his lesser didactic purpose, Sterne's effects are properly subtler. His subject is not the error of man's ways or even their futility; what he is dramatizing, in all good humor, is their comic-pathetic laughableness. Sterne is still willing to be amused by much in man that Swift finds unforgivable.

The qualities of feeling in *Tristram Shandy*, especially the cant critical reading of Sterne as a quack emotionalist, "our Master Sniveller," a virtuoso of the pathétique, need examination and definition. Up to a point, the attitude of the professional sentimentalist, the special "man of feeling," was another of the stock postures Sterne adopted and enjoyed, half theatrically. But his practice was more complex, more artful and more serious, than that of the tearful school of which he is the presumptive father. Sentiment is different from sentimentality, and underneath the fragility and the formality of Sterne's sentiment lies a deep substructure of craft and morality. Options are open to art in deciding how to meet and render the anarchy of experience. And if we are long troubled by the seeming discord between Sterne's pathos and his hilarity, his mourner and his jester, we need to go on to recall their beautiful elision in the ancient comic stock figure of the sad clown of the pantomime, or in the Bitter Fool of Shakespeare. It is an oxymoron that Shakespeare turned to powerful account in the graveyard scene in *Hamlet*, where the dead clown Yorick, the clown who digs graves, and the bitter jester Hamlet come together in a trope of the whole of life. Don Quixote's solemn humorlessness is one way to meet comically the anarchy of experience; Tristram's resolute merriment is another, only slightly less impressive. If we change the expression on the great Don's face, we get the Knight of the Joyful Countenance, who is Tristram. Or perhaps one can imagine an early Picasso *Saltimbanque*, classically calm and romantically attenuated in the original, borrowed and set in ramshackle motion. Thackeray complained that Sterne "paints his face, puts on his ruff and motley clothes, and lays down his carpet and tumbles on it." But Sterne's antic disposition, ravishing in itself, is also a means to a profounder comic purpose.

Sterne's most characteristic passages of pure sentiment seem to me quite invulnerable to honest attack. They are drenched with feeling, but the emotion is so densely motivated, so firmly grounded in established facts of character, so controlled by dramatic context, that we have no right to call it sentimental. Much of this matter, great and small, centers appropriately about my uncle Toby. Tristram, aged ten, watches Toby liberate a fly:

> . . . I'll not hurt thee, says my uncle *Toby*, rising from his chair, and going across the room with the fly in his hand,—I'll not hurt a hair of thy head:—Go, says he, lifting up the sash, and opening his hand as he spoke, to let it escape;—go poor Devil, get thee gone, why should I hurt thee?—This world surely is wide enough to hold both thee and me.

Why should we doubt him, or find the sentiment false or trivial, when the mature Tristram says, ". . . the lesson of universal good-will then taught and imprinted by my uncle *Toby*, has never since been worn out of my mind . . . I often think that I owe one half of my philanthropy to that one accidental impression"? "My heart stops me," Tristram says later, "to pay to thee . . . the tribute I owe thy goodness," and he falls on his knees to vow,

> Whilst I am worth [a shilling], to pay a weeder,—thy path from thy door to thy bowling-green shall never be grown up.—Whilst there is a rood and a half of land in the *Shandy* family, thy fortifications, my dear uncle *Toby*, shall never be demolished.

With his siege-play and his naive amours, Toby has not ceased to be a comic object, and he has not descended to be a sentimental object; but his goodness is indeed of a kind to stop the heart, and Tristram can fall on his knees before it with no shame to himself or to us. The relationship of Uncle Toby and Corporal Trim is one of the funniest and one of the most beautiful in literature. Master and man are "alike subject to overflowings," and their vulnerability to strong feeling is at once part of their comedy and part of their deep human meaning: Sterne does not allow us to separate the laughter and the meaning. They are "two noddles," in Walter Shandy's indulgent phrase, but when Tristram brings the three together in the rich emotion of his prefiguring vision of the funeral of Toby it is hard not to be moved toward wholly honest tears, which we shed as much for the race as for three brilliantly documented archetypes of its tragi-comedy:

> . . . I look towards the velvet pall, decorated with the military ensigns of thy master—he first—the foremost of created beings;—where, I shall see thee, faithful servant! laying his sword and scabbard with a trembling hand across his coffin, and then returning pale as ashes to the door, to take his mourning horse by the bridle, to follow his hearse, as he directed thee;—where—all my father's systems shall be baffled by his sorrows; and, in spite of his philosophy, I shall behold him, as he inspects the lacquered plate, twice taking his spectacles from off his nose, to wipe away the dew which nature has shed upon them—When I see him cast in the rosemary with an air of disconsolation, which cries through my ears,—O *Toby*! in what corner of the world shall I seek thy fellow?

But Sterne's denials of sentiment may be harder to accept than his assertions of sentiment. He moves us by closing a chapter with a feeling passage on time and mutability,

> . . . Time wastes too fast: every letter I trace tells me with what rapidity Life follows my pen; the days and hours of it, more precious, my dear Jenny! than the rubies about thy neck, are flying over our heads like light clouds of a windy day, never to return more—every thing presses on—whilst thou art twisting that lock,—see! it grows grey; and every time I kiss thy hand to bid adieu, and every absence which follows it, are preludes to that eternal separation which we are shortly to make.—
> —Heaven have mercy upon us both!

Then he attacks us with a following chapter of one sentence: "Now, for what the world thinks of that ejaculation—I would not give a groat." If he means that he means it in spite of what the world may think, that is one thing; if he means that he never meant it, then we have been perversely led into an honest emotion and rudely insulted there. Fortunately Sterne is not often so crude or equivocal. But repeatedly, and in some of his most important episodes, he does wilfully complicate and qualify the created emotion. Sterne's greatest scenes of orchestrated pathos, such as the death of Le Fever, Trim's reading of Yorick's sermon on Conscience, or the response of the folk of Shandy Hall to the death of Bobby, are too long to quote and too complex to excerpt satisfactorily. But his method can at least be described.

What Sterne gives us in such episodes is a mingling, or more precisely a plaiting, of several strands of emotion: first the dominant pathetic, next the alternative farcical, finally the recessive tragic—so protectively colored that it is almost invisible. The pathetic, highly formalized, is advanced first, and moves unopposed to what should be a climax, then it is sharply undercut by the farcical. We are left holding a comedy that is exciting and disturbing because it is so expert and apparently so heartless. We can stop there suspended, or we can go back to the first mood and insist on being moved by pathos. Either way we remain uneasy: we feel that we have been moved more complexly than can be explained by either attitude, or by the two in combination. When we face the inadequacy of the ready responses, and ask why Sterne feels this strange need to make game of our stock sadness, we begin to understand the work of the recessive third strand, third color. Its function is frankly to address the fact that our racial sadness is indeed standard stuff: illness, madness, want, war, unkindness, death, every form of frustration great and small, all these are comically and tragically true. How trite, how funny, and how sad they are is the thing nearly impossible to say. I think it is this barely speakable truth that is not so much spoken as pantomimed in the intricate irony of these scenes. Your water is a sore decayer of your whoreson dead body: the explicit courage of the tragic vision is implicit in the "expert" comedy of Sterne.

There is some truth in Ernest Nevin Dilworth's judgment

that in such scenes death is "a kind of wash, and anything but sombre." But if he means that Sterne's purpose is frivolous, he is very wrong. Death may not be sombre in *Tristram Shandy*, but it is none the less real and fatal, thoroughly serious. The point is that it is serious as a part of a wilfully comic complex addressed to the fatality of experience. As Parson Yorick lies dying, he invites his friend Eugenius to inspect his bruised and misshapen head, which no mitre can fit; he speaks his last words "with something of a *cervantic* tone," and as he speaks his friend can see "a stream of lambent fire lighted up for a moment in his eyes." *Tristram Shandy* is a big jest energetic with passion. Both the comedy and the fatality are true. Neither negates the other. Both participate in one organism, which is the image of life. But the text itself gives us the best of metaphors for understanding Sterne's comic management of serious subject, Tristram's description of Yorick's funeral sermon upon Le Fever, which "seems to have been his favourite composition":

> It is upon mortality; and is tied length-ways and crossways with a yarn thrum, and then rolled up and twisted round with a half sheet of dirty blue paper, which seems to have been once the cast cover of a general review, which to this day smells horribly of horse drugs.

All the elements are there, and in due relationship: the fatal subject; the anarchic event ordered in the web of artifice; the whole confined in the envelope of art; the characteristic air of it all determined by the pervading blatant and incongruous aroma.

"Every thing in this world, said my father, is big with jest, —and has wit in it, and instruction too,—if we can but find it out." Sterne has chosen to find the disastrous landscape pregnant with jest, and we must find the instruction as well as the entertainment in his wit. We can uncover the heart of the moral argument, and review the governing comic method, in a great dialogue between the brothers Shandy on the subject of man's trials and how they may be borne. Walter Shandy sets the subject:

> But I say, *Toby*, when one runs over the catalogue of all the cross reckonings and sorrowful *items* with which the heart of man is overcharged, 'tis wonderful by what hidden resources the mind is enabled to stand it out, and bear itself up, as it does against the impositions laid upon our nature.

Toby answers straight in terms of faith (which Walter has dismissed earlier as "*Grangousier's* solution"): " 'Tis by the assistance of Almighty God, cried my uncle *Toby*, . . . we are upheld by the grace and the assistance of the best of Beings." Now Tristram pauses for a stage-direction aside to the reader, addressed as "your connoisseurship," describing in detail his father's histrionic posture in argument, like "that in which *Socrates* is so finely painted by *Raffael* in his school of *Athens*. . . ." The brothers pursue the question:

> Though man is of all others the most curious vehicle, said my father, yet at the same time 'tis of so slight a frame and so totteringly put together, that the sudden jerks and hard jostlings it unavoidably meets with in this hard journey, would overset and tear it to pieces a dozen times a day—was it not, brother *Toby*, that there is a secret spring within us—Which spring, said my uncle *Toby*, I take to be Religion.—Will that set my child's nose on? cried my father, letting go his finger, and striking one hand against the other.—It makes every thing straight for us, answered my uncle *Toby*—Figuratively speaking, dear *Toby*, it may, for aught I know, said my father; but the spring I am speaking of, is that great and elastic power within us of counterbalancing evil, which like a secret spring in a well-ordered machine though it can't prevent the shock—at least it imposes upon our sense of it.

And the scene ends in farce, with Walter Shandy resolving to offset the catastrophe to his son's nose by applying the "magic bias" of a great name: "I must counteract and undo it with the greatest good. He shall be christened *Trismegistus*, brother." "I wish it may answer," says Toby, "rising up": the absurdity is too great even for *Lillabullero*.

Perhaps we can identify the secret spring that sustains the ramshackle human vehicle in one last appropriately curious metaphor. In the masterly little scene that crowns the shambles that mischance has made of Tristram's birth, Dr. Slop, whose *tire-tête* has done the damage, has crept downstairs to the kitchen to attempt some patchwork. Trim sees and reports to the parlor that the man-midwife is "busy making a bridge." Uncle Toby's military infatuation is absolute, and it is no trouble at all for his mind to leap sublimely to the assumption that Dr. Slop "was making a model for the Marquis *d'Hopital's* bridge." Toby's delusion opens the way for a promising peroration by Walter Shandy; but "*Trim's* answer . . . tore the laurel from his brows, and twisted it to pieces":

> God bless your honour, cried *Trim*, 'tis a bridge for master's nose.—In bringing him into the world with his vile instruments, he has crushed his nose, *Susannah* says, as flat as a pancake to his face, and he is making a false bridge with a piece of cotton and a thin piece of whalebone out of *Susannah's* stays, to raise it up.

I suggest that such is the serious mission of Sterne's gaudy work, and of any comic work of his inclusiveness of moral view and brilliance of means. With its grand beggarly tools it builds a bridge to sustain us over the tragic gap between the real and the ideal as well as over the comic gap between the normal and the extravagant. Like tragedy, great comedy can give us the purgative spectacle of dignity addressed to fate. Its act of will and of passion is a form of the secret spring, that great and elastic power within us, and it finds its sources and its voice in an undismayed love of life.